Rules and laws in sociology

Methodological Perspectives

A series edited by Richard J. Hill
University of Oregon

Rules and law in sociology

edited by **Robert Brown**
Institute of Advanced Studies
Australian National University

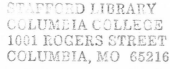 Aldine Publishing Company / *Chicago*

About the editor

Robert Brown is Senior Fellow, Philosophy Department, at the
Institute of Advanced Studies, Australian National University.
He was educated at the University of New Mexico, the University
of Chicago, and the University of London, where he received his
Ph.D. in 1952. He has taught at Los Angeles State College, the
University of Wisconsin, the University of Massachusetts, and
Amherst, and is editor of the *Australasian Journal of Philosophy*
and consulting editor to the *Journal for the Theory of Social
Behavior*. He has edited *Between Hume and Mill*, co-edited
Contemporary Philosophy in Australia, written the volume
Explanation in Social Science, and contributed several dozen
articles to professional journals.

*First U.S. edition published 1973 by
Aldine Publishing Company
529 South Wabash Avenue
Chicago, Illinois 60605*

*English edition published by
Routledge & Kegan Paul Ltd.
London*

*Library of Congress Catalog Card Number 72–96602
ISBN 0–202–30257–1*

Printed in Great Britain

Contents

Preface

In this book I discuss, and propose answers to, a set of closely related problems in sociological investigation. The four main elements of the set are indicated by the way in which the chapters are grouped: the first two chapters are concerned with *definitions*; the second two with *properties*; the next two with *generalizations*; and the final three with *explanations and conclusions*. Every social scientist must cope with the problems which these topics raise, and at least some philosophers also find them interesting. I try to bring out here a number of the many important relationships that hold among the four of them. In particular, I try to make clear the consequences, for both sociological generalization and explanation, of the sociologist's adopting certain kinds of definitions or of utilizing certain sorts of properties.

It is reasonable to ask why I concentrate, in the first five chapters, on the work of so few authors: for example, Blalock and Srole. 'Why', it might well be asked, 'do you not try to obtain a much better sample of the work of contemporary sociologists? If you had done that—if you had quoted the texts of a wide range of sociologists—you would have given your readers the evidence upon which they could have made up their own minds as to the extent and provenance of the defects to which you so often refer. As it is, your comments can be dismissed as applying, at best, to a small, unrepresentative, even unimportant, set of research studies. You have not yourself applied some of the very techniques of surveying and sampling whose absence you lament in others.'

My answer to this query is simple. It is, in brief, that I have not tried, and have not wanted to try, to survey a whole field of study or to indict any of its students. Instead, I have chosen, in some of my chapters, to examine at length the procedures and arguments embodied in the ordinary working papers of several reputable contemporary sociologists. I have tried to avoid choosing either the worst or most brilliant work of its kind. But most of the examples are studies which, quite understandably, have had some influence within their fields. Surely no one would claim, or has claimed, that the work chosen is beneath notice; or that because it has been deliberately drawn from the recent past, it represents a method or style of procedure which is no longer followed today. Many sociologists are now actively working and teaching along lines similar to those discussed here. It is true that I have not shown this to be so, since I have taken the representativeness of my examples not to be in dispute, and hence not to raise any issue of interest. But if my sample were challenged, I should ask to see the body of work which escapes the limitations of some of my examples—escapes in the sense of not merely avoiding their errors but of achieving what they failed to achieve.

In any case, I have tried to use the space and time which a representative survey would require for what seemed to me a more urgent task, that of closely examining, in detail, a few pieces of respectable, and not obviously unrepresentative, sociological investigation. I could as easily have chosen many other examples instead of the present ones, though my procedure, and I think my results, would have remained the same. It should go without saying—though I hasten to say it—that my comments refer to types of arguments and methods of reasoning, and not to the professional abilities of the sociologists whose work has conveniently illustrated that reasoning. It is because of the very considerable abilities of contemporary sociologists, and in particular the abilities of the ones whom I instance, that the difficulties of the field seem to me important. For if these difficulties could be attributed to the inadequate abilities of specific sociologists, rather than to the shortcomings of a widely used procedure, there would be no set of problems worth discussing. It is the discrepancy between the intelligence and effort now being devoted to sociological problems, and the paucity of the results, which lead me to conclude that the problems arise from the practice itself, and not from the idiosyncrasies of its practitioners.

Acknowledgments

I thank Professors Quentin Gibson and John Passmore, Mr Geoffrey Mortimore, and Dr Peter Sheehan for having given so generously of their time in commenting at length on earlier drafts of this book. It is most unlikely that the many changes which I have made as a result of their pointed criticisms will lay all their doubts to rest. It is quite certain, however, that if their doubts had not been expressed, my errors would have multiplied with even less restraint than that which they now display. I am grateful, also, to Miss Janette Paris for her help in reading proofs, and to Mrs Margaret Capper and Miss Isabel Sheaffe for their indispensable typing.

A large portion of the first chapter of this book was first published as 'Policy-Dependent Terms in Sociology: The Case of "Discrimination" ' in *the Australian and New Zealand Journal of Sociology* for October 1971. To its editor, Dr Frank Jones, I owe a number of helpful suggestions. In this same issue there is a comment on my argument by Professor H. M. Blalock. Almost all of section three, chapter seven, has been drawn, substantially unchanged, from my 'Comment' on J. O. Wisdom's paper 'Situational Individualism and Emergent Group-Properties' in *Explanation in the Behavioural Sciences*, edited by Robert Borger and Frank Cioffi, 1970. I thank the publishers, Cambridge University Press, for permission to reprint here. Interested readers will find a reply to me by Professor Wisdom in that volume.

Definitions

Chapter one

Scientific definitions, as the large literature on the subject testifies, can be inadequate to the task at hand in many different ways. But of the definitional difficulties which disturb the work of sociologists, there is one sort of difficulty, and hence one kind of problem, that appears with distressing regularity. Indeed, some critics suggest, in an unjustified tone of relief, that the deficiency arises from the nature of the subject-matter itself. 'Why else', they ask, 'is it so difficult to produce useful criteria of application for terms so basic to sociological thinking as "prejudice", "discrimination", "social deviance", "delinquent", "alienation", "relative deprivation", and many others? Moreover, if the operational rules of application for terms as fundamental as these have still not been settled', the critics continue, 'then there is no hope that the network of secondary terms whose sense is partially dependent on that of the more basic ones can have adequate rules of application either. The results can be only what we find in fact: perpetual confusion about the factors to be described and constant dismay at the triviality of their inter-relationships. What we want, and have tried in vain to find, is a set of terms which we can use precisely and unambiguously to refer to certain measurable properties of theoretical interest. Our obvious inability to produce adequate criteria for applying these terms is strong evidence that the social life of human beings has no such properties. There is simply nothing of the required sort to be defined.'

What the critics complain of here is more important, for our present purpose, than is their diagnosis. Before judging the soundness of the latter, we must examine the basis of the former. Do these troublesome terms have anything in common? Is it true that they are resistant to satisfactory operational criteria? If they are resistant, why should this be so? And does the answer to this last question tell us anything about where we should look—or not look—for theoretically interesting properties? Only if the answers to the first two questions are 'yes', do we have to cope with the next two. For if the former answers are 'no' we have to face the quite different question 'How did such an unjustified complaint ever arise?'

In either case we have an opportunity to try to account for a wide-spread feeling among sociologists that there is a close connection between two familiar problems: that of the definitional recalcitrance of certain terms and that of their absence from lawlike generalizations of any interest. That there is such a connection has yet to be shown; but if there is, its importance will justify the time taken to establish that fact. If there is no such connection, the reasons we have for believing there is none will be a necessary step towards answering the question 'Whatever made us believe that there was?'

1. The problem exemplified

Let us begin with a simple case and work toward a more vexing one. The definition of 'minorities' given by Arnold Rose in the *International Encyclopedia of the Social Sciences* runs as follows:

> a group of people—differentiated from others in the same society by race, nationality, religion, or language—who both think of themselves as a differentiated group and are thought of by the others as a differentiated group with negative connotations. Further, they are relatively lacking in power and hence are subjected to certain exclusions, discriminations, and other differential treatment.

Rose goes on to say that what is vital is

> a set of attitudes—those of group identification from within the group and those of prejudice from without—and a set of behaviours—those of self-segregation from within the group and those of discrimination and exclusion from without.

Now it is immediately clear that the criteria used in the first part of this definition have to be interpreted as not being exhaustive. This is a pardonable fault, but one likely to be noticed by other social scientists. For there are some societies in which there are groups of people who, although they are confined to occupations of low prestige, do not enjoy full political privileges or equal protection of law, and are excluded from the social life of the remainder of the society, are yet of the same race, language, nationality, and religion as those of the members of the majority group. Certain Indian castes are examples of such minorities, or at least have been so in the past. Their members were discriminated against from without and maintained self-segregation by endogamous marriage, for example, from within. So a difference in one or more of these four features—race, nationality, language, or religion—is not a necessary condition of being a minority. And these differences are obviously not sufficient conditions for being a minority group, since in many societies the differences exist in the absence of self-segregation and prejudice. Moreover, not all numerical minorities are subject to discrimination. The most that can be said is that discriminators commonly explain and justify their actions by referring to such differences when these happen to be present. When they are not, any difference between members of the dominant and subordinate groups may be seized upon as required, and today some quite imaginary differences are giving good service in support of discriminatory treatment.

The reason why it is useful to emphasize the obvious fact that any difference will serve to justify discrimination against a minority is this: a characteristic mentioned in a definition may be merely an accompanying feature of the definiendum; that is, a feature whose relation to the defining properties is contingent and not exceptionless. Nevertheless, it may be important to refer to this accompanying characteristic in the definition. It may be important because the feature in question can serve as a useful identifying marker, even though it cannot always be relied on to indicate the presence of the definiendum. Thus it is useful to know that a minority group is quite commonly, even although not necessarily, different in race, nationality, religion, or language from the majority in a society. For it is often much easier for an observer to discover these differences than it is for him to find out whether there is a social group which is numerically less than half, lacking in power, and subject to discriminatory treatment. Social groups which discriminate against certain minorities have an interest in not advertising the fact, whereas such differences as those of race and religion are not only more difficult to conceal, but to many people there seems to be no particular reason why they should be concealed. Race, religion, nationality, and language, therefore, offer the investigator a likely starting point in his study of discriminatory practices against a minority group. Any definition of 'minorities' which failed to mention such probable indicators would fail to direct our attention properly. For one of the chief tasks of a scientific definition is to enable the scientist to locate and recognize that which is being defined. The fact that the usual indicators cannot always be relied on is no reason why they cannot sometimes be used to advantage. The same considerations hold of any other difference, real or imaginary, which is employed to justify discriminatory treatment. But in knowing this much the investigator also knows that the existence of a minority group does not depend upon the presence of any specific difference between it and the majority.

The defining properties of a minority group, according to Rose's

5

definition, are these: discrimination, prejudice, and exclusion by the dominant group, and self-segregation by the subordinate one. Is there anything objectionable in this characterization? Many critics would argue that there is. 'It embodies', they would say, 'some of the characteristic faults of definitions produced by social scientists. It professes to give sufficient and necessary conditions for the definiendum. But when we attempt to apply the definition to actual cases we find that it is useless for the sociologists' purposes, for it does not enable us to recognize any given instance of a minority group. We are supposed, for example, to use the presence of discrimination as one of the means of picking out a minority group. Yet the definition of "discrimination" given by sociologists is itself no more helpful than that of "minority group". The two definitions are equally unsatisfactory, since neither provides us with any practical way of locating actual cases. We can no more recognize instances of discrimination by using the definition provided by sociologists than we can recognize examples of minority groups by means of Rose's definition. Yet no one suggests that these two terms are purely theoretical ones to which no operational tests are directly relevant. But if the terms are supposed to refer to observable aspects of social life, the definitions of such terms ought to allow us to pick out examples of the properties to which they refer.'

Anyone sympathetic to this criticism might conclude with the following diagnosis: 'The defects complained of here can arise from three different sources. The first is that the criteria put forward in these and many other definitions are not clearly enough stated: the criteria are vague, ambiguous, inconsistent, and thus not open to useful measurement. Second, there is the fact that independently of whether or not the criteria are clearly stated, they do not have many recognizable instances; clarity and consistency of criteria are not sufficient to ensure that in practice they can be applied to cases. Third, and independently of the other two sources of complaint, there is the fact that the criteria do not isolate those features which concern the sociologist; a definition can have all virtues but that of pointing to the particular characteristic which bears importantly upon his work. Because sociologists do not distinguish these three kinds of inadequacy, the source of their definitional problems remains obscure. But if we examine what some sociologists themselves have said about the problems of defining such terms as "discrimination", we shall find that all three types of defect play an unfortunate role in the discussions.'

Contrary to this diagnosis, it will be argued later that the real source of the problems associated with 'discrimination' and 'prejudice' lies elsewhere, and that as a result of neglecting this additional source of his definitional difficulties, the sociologist sometimes tries

6

to measure what it is logically impossible to measure. This conceptual confusion can only be avoided by close scrutiny of the link between inadequate definition and unsatisfactory investigation. One simple way of doing this is to look, in some detail, at specifically sociological attempts to define 'prejudice' and 'discrimination', and to look, also, at certain more general questions which arise from the attempt to give operationally useful criteria of application for various other terms. Some of these, like 'prejudice' and 'discrimination', belong to a distinctive and recalcitrant class. But before discussing the special problem associated with this class of terms, it will be necessary to consider certain more obvious defects of the definitions of these terms, defects which fall within the three types just given.

What, then, are these defects? They are referred to in the critics' complaint that the properties listed in the definition raise the same problems which the definition was supposed to solve, and that the answer has merely been postponed. That this complaint has some justification can easily be seen. For 'prejudice' has been defined by Otto Klineberg in the *International Encyclopedia of the Social Sciences* as 'an unsubstantiated prejudgment of an individual or group, favourable or unfavourable in character, tending to action in a consonant direction'. This definition resembles, in part, the entry in the *O.E.D.*: 'a judgment formed before due examination or consideration . . . a preconceived opinion . . . an unreasoning predilection or objection.' However, neither definition is very helpful. Sociologists claim to be interested in prejudiced judgments when these judgments have as their targets certain groups of people, groups commonly identified by means of their race, religion, nationality, language, and —we can add—culture. But why should sociologists find 'unsubstantiated prejudgments' and 'preconceived opinions' about such groups of any *scientific* interest? Unconsidered judgments and unreasoning objections form the bulk of our views, and it is difficult to imagine how it could be otherwise. We do not have the time or energy to withhold all our judgments until they have passed critical scrutiny. And in any case, it is logically impossible that all our judgments should be formed with due examination. For if we did not make some of them uncritically—placing initial trust, for example, in our senses and memory—we could make no judgments at all. We should be caught in a vicious infinite regress generated by our attempt to make our very first judgment.

No one expects a child to give 'due examination' to all the opinions which he absorbs. Yet both Klineberg's definition and the *O.E.D.* entry suggest that, in general, both children and adults are remiss. Both of them form most of their judgments and beliefs before due consideration; they accept uncritically, for example, the pronouncements of authorities. And even if by later examination someone corrects his earlier view, this process of correction does not offer us a method of avoiding the formation of prejudiced judgments in the first place. So the effect of these definitions is to classify the great majority of our judgments about people under the label 'prejudices'. If this is a useful and accurate definition of 'prejudice', then social scientists have little reason to be concerned with the study of social prejudices as such. For if most of our judgments are prejudiced ones, then our judgments about social groups present no special problem. Views based on prejudice will be what we ought to expect to find everywhere, and it may be that the presence of some unprejudiced judgments toward social groups will be rare enough to require explanation. Of course, in that situation it will still be sensible to ask why prejudiced views are so common, but then we shall also be assuming that social prejudices are so common because *most* judgments are prejudiced. Thus the question which is of interest to social scientists will have been altered, since what is now taken by them to be the usual state of affairs will no longer be so.

However, for the purposes of sociologists there is another defect of these definitions of 'prejudice'. Not only do they fail to distinguish the class of prejudiced judgments from the wider class of mere unsupported and unexamined judgments, but they neglect to mention the sociologically important feature of all prejudiced opinions: their *unreasonable retention* in the face of countervailing evidence or argument. For the sociologist, an unsupported judgment that is responsive to rational criticism cannot have been held only as a prejudice. If we said that it was, we should be extending the application of the word 'prejudice' so widely as to make it useless for marking the very class of cases in which we are chiefly interested as social scientists. This class consists of adverse beliefs, impervious to correction by rational argument alone, concerning the members of given social groups. If initially unsupported beliefs came to be rationally defended later by their proponents, we might still think the views mistaken but we could not as sociologists correctly say that at first they had been mere 'prejudices'. For their presence would not generate the basic scientific question which arises concerning prejudices. Suppose, for example, we wondered why some Europeans dislike all members of the group which they refer to as 'orientals'. We should only have to learn that these Europeans mistakenly believe all 'orientals' to be dirty, dishonest, and diseased in order to be in a position to correct the belief and thus remove the prejudice. The fact that the belief turns out to be incorrigible is what creates the scientific problem, namely, why, in the teeth of all evidence and rational argument, the belief is retained.

A prejudiced belief, then, is not, for sociological purposes, to be defined as one which is unsupported by evidence and rational argument, but as one which is irrationally argument-resistant. A brilliant guess or hunch need not be regarded as a prejudice even though the confirming evidence is long delayed. It is only if the agent clings to such a hunch despite his knowledge of strong disconfirming evidence that his objectivity becomes suspect. Moreover, the reason why irrational retention should be taken as the sociologically important property of prejudice has already been suggested. It is that only the presence of this property creates the problem with which scientific studies of prejudice are concerned.

When a sociologist investigates what he calls 'prejudiced beliefs' he has already accepted the view that the beliefs in question are held unreasonably. Of course they need not be adverse beliefs. It is merely that favourable prejudices about social groups—for example, that all Englishmen are honest—do not usually present the practical problems which are generated by unfavourable prejudices. But in principle the former might be as disruptive of a society's activities as are the latter. A tribe which persisted in believing, against all reason, that its European enemies were so honest that they could not be bought off by native gold might owe its disappearance to this prejudiced admiration.

It is important that the sociologist be clear as to whether he takes the unreasonable beliefs he is investigating to be unreasonable because non-rationally or irrationally formed, or unreasonable because non-rationally or irrationally retained. If he does not pause to draw this elementary distinction (*between unreasoning acquisition and unreasonable retention*), the questions he asks about prejudices are likely to lead to confused and inconclusive answers. In addition, this ambiguity of definition will infect any other terms in whose definitions 'prejudiced belief' plays a part. Any definition of 'minority groups', for example, which includes prejudice by the dominant group as a defining property, will be defective. For since the recognition of any given case of prejudice will not be straight-forward, neither will it be easy to recognize the existence of any particular minority group. So the failure to define 'prejudiced belief' unambiguously will have, as a result, our inability either to recognize or adequately describe a minority group by using this criterion.

2. Residential clustering and social segregation

However, Rose gives prejudice by a dominant group as only one of the defining properties of a minority group; the other properties are exclusion, or discrimination by the dominant group, and self-segregation by the subordinate one. But the role of these properties in the definition of 'minority group' is by no means simple, for socio-logical discussions of their use raise a number of characteristic problems which are both interesting in themselves and important for the consequences of their answers. Let us first take the case of segregation–exclusion, and then, somewhat later, that of discrimination.

Sociologists are usually interested in the properties displayed by groups of people rather than in the personality traits of individual persons. Expressions like 'degree of prejudice', 'residential segregation' and 'minority-discrimination' are taken to refer to group-properties. The sociologist's first task is often thought to be that of characterizing these in such a way that they can be measured while yet preserving the intended sense of their names. Thus in his book, *Toward a Theory of Minority-Group Relations*,[1] H. M. Blalock considers certain problems in the measurement of two properties, residential segregation and minority discrimination. He begins by asking how we can measure the degree of residential segregation exhibited by a given group. The first step of his answer to this question is to assert that 'The notions of no segregation and complete segregation are, of course, reasonably simple.' For 'whenever the minority is distributed evenly' throughout a census-tract (or other unit) there is no segregation. He continues thus:[2]

> In contrast, there is complete segregation whenever all members of the minority are separated from all members of the dominant group, so that all tracts contain members of one group only. Ambiguities occur, however, in specifying criteria for measuring intermediate degrees of segregation.

Now it is immediately obvious that the determination of degrees of segregation by the method of evenness of distribution is a complicated process. The difficulty, much discussed by social scientists, is that our results will alter with the size and shape of our geographical or census units. If a given tract is large enough it may contain residential clusters which are themselves the result of discriminatory housing practices. Yet since they occur within the tract they will not be counted as segregated units. In some section of some cities, for example, adjoining streets are occupied by different ethnic groups. If we take each of the streets as an individual census unit, then there is a high degree of segregation within those neighbourhoods. But if we take the neighbourhoods as our units, the degree of segregation is low. This dependence of degree of segregation upon the size and shape of the census unit makes it clear that we must have some other method of determining residential segregation than by mere geographical clustering. That is, one of the common, and sociological, uses of the term 'residentially segregated' has written into it the independent assumption that the clustering is either produced or

[1] New York, 1967.   [2] P. 12.

10

maintained by discriminatory practices. The other and more general sense of 'segregation', in which the word simply means 'geographically separated by residence', is not in itself relevant here. Sociologists are also concerned with mere geographical clustering, of course, even when it is the result of people living together merely because they believe themselves to have important features in common, e.g. an interest in horses. But sociologists *are* especially concerned with residential clustering when it is a *sign* of social segregation. This is the sense of 'segregation' which *Webster's Dictionary* gives as: 'the separation or isolation of a race, class, or ethnic group by enforced or voluntary residence in a restricted area, barriers to social intercourse, divided educational facilities, or other discriminatory means.' Leo Kuper has characterized this kind of segregation as 'an institutionalised form of social distance expressed in physical separation', whether the separation is 'compulsory or voluntary, deliberate or spontaneous'.[1]

Hence, if we are to preserve the notion of social distance and institutionalized avoidance which is of interest to sociologists, we must concentrate on the second, or discriminatory, sense of 'segregation'. That is, we must be able to identify the geographical separation of the group as a segregation whose origin or maintenance is produced by social discrimination. The separation need not be imposed by force or maintained by fraud: for example, the separation may be adopted voluntarily by the subordinate group as a defensive measure; or a minority with power and prestige may discriminate against a majority group. How, then, can we distinguish in any given case between mere geographical clustering, whether based on income, tastes, or culture, and discriminatory segregation? For once we concede that a minority can react to the behaviour of the majority by spontaneously withdrawing to its own residential areas, we can no longer discover the cause of the clustering simply by finding evidence of *enforced* isolation. Actual enforcement by one group may be unnecessary if the other group is co-operative; or each group may discriminate against the other. Furthermore, a group may become socially segregated, over a period of time, even if it has not deliberately or spontaneously set itself apart, and even if it has not knowingly been set apart by the majority. From an accident of physical isolation, an original part of the community may become socially isolated and then discriminated against, though perhaps rather slowly. No one may have intended or desired this result initially, but circumstances may produce it as an unintended consequence. And once established, the segregation may be maintained either as deliberate policy or by mere customary practice.

Clearly, the discriminatory sense of 'residential segregation' is the

[1] 'Segregation', *International Encyclopedia of the Social Sciences*, p. 144.

more important one in studies of prejudice. Yet sociologists themselves occasionally neglect this point. Blalock, for example, writes that there is 'a fundamental difference between the concept of discrimination and that of segregation'. It is, he says, that discrimination 'must be measured indirectly, thus necessitating a set of theoretical assumptions—many of which will be untestable—in order to link the notion of discrimination to actual measures'[1] whereas segregation can be measured directly. However, this supposed difference between the two concepts certainly cannot be a difference between *discriminatory* segregation and discrimination, since the former is defined as segregation either initiated or maintained by the latter. Hence if it is true that discrimination must be measured indirectly and requires untestable theoretical assumptions, then these difficulties will also arise in the case of discriminatory segregation. For to be able to measure the amount of discriminatory segregation present in a given area is the same as to be able to measure the contribution made by discrimination to residential clustering. If this procedure is to be called an indirect means of measuring discrimination, it is also a logically necessary step in the measurement of discriminatory segregation. Thus the latter cannot be directly measurable when the former is not.

On the other hand, the fundamental difference cannot be that between mere residential clustering and discrimination. For not only would this difference be of no sociological interest, but in any obvious sense of the phrase 'directly and indirectly measurable', discrimination sometimes is directly measurable and residential clustering sometimes is not. Both situations are exemplified in the case of a city-state whose official policy is to discriminate against a suspected but secret Christian minority, the members of which in fact live clustered together unknown to the majority. Here it cannot reasonably be objected that the problem of identifying minority members is merely a practical one, that if we had additional sources of information we could count the Christians and thus directly measure the extent of their residential clustering. For the same can be said of covert discriminators, given that we have a criterion of discrimination. If we had access to their diaries or to their private conversations, we should equally be able to directly measure the extent of the discrimination by counting discriminators. The fact that we often cannot identify discriminators because they prefer to remain anonymous, and that we often can identify the members of residential clusters because they cannot remain anonymous, is simply a convenient accident.

Since, then, the measurement of discriminatory segregation and the measurement of discrimination proper raise much the same kinds

[1] *Op. cit.*, p. 15.

of problems, we can now ask what grounds there are for believing, as Blalock does, that the definition and measurement of discrimination require 'a theory of social causation' which, in part at least, is untestable.

3. The concept of discrimination

Blalock begins by saying that it is difficult to define 'discrimination' briefly and usefully. For definitions like 'it is the unequal treatment of equals merely because of their minority characteristics' introduce the following problem. Assume that discrimination consists in the differential treatment of a person merely because of his supposed membership in a subordinate group. How, asks Blalock, can we find out whether his treatment is actually caused by his supposed membership? To know this we should have to know that the treatment was *not* due to a host of other factors like social class or amount of income.[1]

> Is the employer who selects white graduates in preference to Negroes discriminating? To claim that this is the case requires one to demonstrate that college graduates of the two races have had equivalent training and have performed at the same levels. Few persons who know anything at all about differences among colleges would be so rash as to make this claim.

We can make the definition fuller and more precise, but that by itself will not satisfy the objector. The *Random House Dictionary* defines 'discrimination' as 'treatment or consideration of, or making a distinction in favour of or against, a person or thing based on the group, class or category to which that person or thing belongs rather than on individual merit'. Clearly, this definition must be supplemented by some phrase like 'when such treatment is supposed to take merit as decisive'. Without such a qualification we do not rule out cases in which *only* categorical distinctions are relevant to treatment. If I favour a starving man over his starving cow, 'Betsey', I favour him merely because he is a man, not because his individual merit is greater than the individual merit of Betsey. *Any* human being, most human beings would say, should be favoured, in such circumstances, over *any* animal. Even given this qualification, however, we might still find it difficult to discover, in any particular instance, whether discrimination was present—that is, whether treatment was based on category or on individual merit.

Blalock's objection thus takes a form of the complaint described earlier: some sociological definitions may or may not state the necessary and sufficient conditions for a concept, but they give us no

[1] *Op. cit.*, p. 17.

practical means of recognizing instances of it. The absence of such probable indicators sharply decreases the scientific usefulness of a definition, and this, Blalock might say, is the case with the definition of 'discrimination'. For it gives us no clue as to how we might locate instances of discriminatory practices. The fact that similar difficulties crop up in other fields is not helpful. Definitions of such concepts as 1084-poisoning or unconscious envy, and the detection of the early stages of certain well-defined diseases, are troublesome for exactly the same reason that the notion of discrimination is troublesome in sociology.

The conclusion drawn by Blalock is that 'When we attempt to measure discrimination we usually obtain measures of *inequality*, such as differences between white and Negro income or occupational levels.'[1] He goes on to ask why, then, we should not eliminate the concept of discrimination completely and substitute our direct measures of inequality? His answer is that discrimination is a convenient intervening variable. Discrimination stands between the directly measurable independent variables which produce it and the directly measurable inequalities which it produces in turn. As a connecting link, the concept of discrimination has a certain explanatory value even though our measurements of the degree of discrimination present are no more than measurements of the inequalities caused by discrimination.

Taken at face value this objection is perverse. It seems quite clear how we come to recognize particular examples of discrimination once we are familiar with the concept. Discriminators, when they feel secure, *tell* us what they have done, are doing, or intend to do if the occasion arises. Or they *show* this to us by their behaviour. What they say and what they do can reinforce each other strongly. So in order for us ever to know, or show, that an employer is discriminating against Negro applicants we do not always have to know, or show, that their training and performance is equivalent to those of other applicants. We have only to find out that the employer, whether intentionally, deliberately, or through unconscious desire, made it more difficult for Negroes to be employed (merely because they were taken to be Negroes) than for non-Negroes. It obviously does not matter how we find this out—whether by wire-tapping his orders or by photographing his confidential memoranda. Nor does it matter whether the employer is himself prejudiced against Negroes. It is only what he does in his capacity as an employer of labour that is relevant to the charge of discriminatory hiring. Many such practices live on because a large number of people believe that other influential people will object to their elimination. It is thus theoretically possible that in a community without a single prejudiced person, discrimination

[1] *Ibid.*

14

might exist simply because many people falsely believed prejudice to exist.

Clearly, if we discovered that of 100 Chicago companies tested by such direct methods, 68 hired few Negroes over a given period of time, we should have begun the direct measurement of the discrimination being practised by Chicago's employers. This would be much more useful information to us than if we simply were to learn that in those same 100 firms 68 employed very few Negroes. For we should still have to find out why this was so. The reason why Blalock pessimistically asks, 'How can we know on any given occasion that a particular employer is discriminating against negroes?', is that he has in mind the characteristic situation of ignorance in which the sociologist so often finds himself. He possesses certain information, for example, about the relatively small number of Negroes employed as aircraft pilots on commercial flights. But he does not know whether this is due to a shortage of qualified Negroes or to covert policy on the part of the airlines. Since the latter piece of information is not available to him, he investigates the former question. Suppose he discovers that of a substantial number of apparently qualified applicants, few were chosen. He has then to determine whether there is racially discriminatory hiring as a result of policy, or whether there is low employment because of poor qualifications, or whether some other factor is present.

It is perfectly reasonable, therefore, that in the absence of his ability to apply direct tests for the existence of discrimination in the people suspected of it, the sociologist should turn to indirect tests. He tries to determine from the differences between various sets of figures what proportion of the differences is due to racial discrimination. This difficult method of inferring discrimination he then comes to think of as the common and natural way of measuring the degree of discrimination present. He also comes to think that the chief practical problem is that of obtaining reliable and consistent measures of inequality. And he is then led to ask, as a serious question, what unit of discrimination these measures refer to: acts, agents, or victims?[1] The answer to this last question, obviously, is that it depends on the problem to be solved. In the case of the Chicago employers we are interested in measuring the proportion of discriminating agents among the total population of actors. But if we were studying the activity of a single firm we might be interested in finding out how often, in a given period of time, that company had discriminated against Negro applicants for jobs. We should then be interested in determining the number of discriminatory *acts* and what proportion they were of the total number of actions taken on all applicants.

[1] Cf. Blalock, *op. cit.*, p. 17n.

At this point we should remind ourselves that the original objection has not yet been met. The objection was that many sociological definitions, including that of 'discrimination', provide no practical test for recognizing examples and for correctly using the terms so defined. The reply to this has been that there is, in fact, a direct and practical test for locating discriminators. We ask them, and they either tell us or unequivocally show us the answer. If there were not some simple test available, it is difficult to imagine how our present concept of discrimination could have developed. Nevertheless, it is still true that our test is not provided by—described in—our own definition. And this point is of practical importance. For if discriminators become wary and secretive in the future, our simple test will no longer work. We shall have a concept of discrimination and no way of applying it to actual cases. Hence there is good reason for us to try to alter our definition so as to make it include some reference to a serviceable test: that is, to refer to a property which is both identifiable by scientifically acceptable means and a reliable indicator of discrimination.

The first question, therefore, is this. In the absence of direct information from employers, does the detection of discriminatory hiring require us to demonstrate that applicants of all competing groups 'have had equivalent training and have performed at the same levels'?

If the hiring has already taken place, and if all direct methods such as confession, testimony by spectators, and eavesdropping are ruled out, then the answer is obviously 'yes'. The only relevant pieces of information left to us are the figures which show the disproportionate failure of minority applicants, their comparative qualifications, and their past performance. But we need not often be in this desperate position for very long. All we need do in order to establish the presence of such a hiring procedure is to make some tests in which minority membership is unknown to the employer. Then we can compare his choices with those made after he knew the minority membership of the applicant.

Of course the form which these experiments take will vary with the case. If we believe that an employer will hire *any* white person who is able-bodied and *no* Negro irrespective of his qualifications, our task is simple. We disguise our Negro applicants as whites and we disguise our white applicants as Negroes. We shall soon collect the required information. But if we suspect that hiring standards for Negroes have been set higher than those for whites, so that proportionately fewer Negroes are accepted, we still need not demonstrate equivalence of training and performance in order to demonstrate that the standards of acceptance differ. We can divide the candidates, at random, into two groups, one for which racial membership is known and the other

16

for which racial membership is unknown. By comparing the acceptance rates for the two groups, any bias of standards will be revealed. If an employer raises his standards for *all* applicants whose race is unknown, that too will be revealed by the acceptance rates and will requtre explanation by him.

Now to some of these suggestions it will immediately be replied that they concede the point at issue, for while they do not require us to *demonstrate* equivalence of training and performance, does not their success, in any but the simplest case, *assume* such equivalence? Unless the anonymous members of the competing groups actually had equivalent qualifications, we should have no way of finding out whether an inequality was due to discrimination or to a difference in qualifications. Therefore, in order to demonstrate the soundness of our suggested tests we should have first to demonstrate that they fulfilled the equivalence conditions.

However, this reply misses the point. Our randomization procedure *alone*, without demonstration of equivalent training and performance, will eliminate gross differences of qualification between the competing groups, and if in any given situation the procedure does not do so, we can easily arrange further tests that will. For example, we can give counterfeit but similar records to selected Negro and white applicants whose race is known to the employer. Or we can issue counterfeit records which favour the Negro group. The only assumption being made here is that we know what the employer will count as equivalent qualifications. If we do not know that much we are in no position to suggest that he may be practising discrimination. And if we do know what will count as equivalent qualifications, the various tests available to us will make it unnecessary, except in the case of confidential decisions in the past, to demonstrate actual equivalence of training and performance.

Yet this answer is only the first step toward the solution of our larger problem, namely, how we might go about the task of altering our definition of 'discrimination' so as to make it incorporate some reference to a useful test. And here we must remember that the most useful sort of test, as far as the sociologist is concerned, will be one which allows him both to locate discriminatory practices and to measure their extent. Recognition of such practices is essential. But the sociologist's next question is how to measure them. Because social inequalities can be measured directly, there is a strong temptation to substitute their measurement for that of discrimination on the ground that measurement of the latter is either impractical or, worse, logically obscure. And while we have rejected the view that it is impractical to detect discriminatory practices other than by demonstrating actual equivalence of qualifications, our arguments, if correct, show only that such a demonstration is not a *necessary*

17

element in a serviceable test. They do not rule out the possibility that such a demonstration, giving hiring inequalities, is sufficient as a test, although there are also other sufficient tests: for example, eavesdropping.

Chapter two

1. The principle of probable indicators

Blalock's suggestion was that actual equivalence of qualifications is difficult to establish and, hence, that the presence of such equivalence is not a practical test for the existence of discrimination. But since we need only *simulated* equivalence for a test, it is a reasonable question whether equivalence of training and performance is not one of the sufficient tests to which a useful definition of 'discrimination' might refer, explicitly or implicitly. How well would such an equivalence-condition work?

Suppose that an employer is an American Negro of working-class origin who hires only non-Negroes. His private reason for doing this is that he believes, rightly or wrongly, that Negro applicants, for the most part, will be jealous of his success and thus will not work well for him. Although his employment policy is not influenced by any dislike of Negroes for other reasons, it *is* influenced by his belief that the American Negroes he might hire will behave unacceptably toward him as their employer. He takes the property of being an American Negro, given present conditions, to be sufficient ground for not being hired by him. The consequences are much the same as though he refused to employ American Negroes merely because they were Negroes. Is it, however, a policy based on racial discrimination?

Many people would answer 'no' without hesitation. They would say that being a Negro, even an American Negro, was not a major cause of the employer's refusal to hire. The major cause was his belief in the likelihood of the candidates feeling resentful toward him. He did not discriminate against the applicants merely because of their race. He refused to hire them because of a quality which he believed that all his American Negro applicants would tend to display; the connection between being a Negro and being prone to resentment was taken by him to be close but accidental. This could be made clear if we introduced other Negro applicants—perhaps West Indians or Brazilians—whom the employer would not think resentful and thus would be willing to employ.

The obvious difficulty with this reply is that our adoption of the principle on which it relies will force us to accept, without complaint, some apparent cases of discrimination. For the principle is that a person's membership in a certain group or class—for example, a certain ethnic or religious group—is sometimes an accurate sign of his having particular qualities which may be either wanted or unwanted on given occasions. The closeness of the connection between group or class membership and these other qualities is unaffected by the fact that the connection is merely fortuitous, that there is no lawlike association between the two sets of properties. For the purposes of practical men, a reasonably stable but quite accidental connection between such properties is useful enough. A practical man lives by probable indicators, so that if his experience has been that most Swiss are commercially honest and most Americans are not, he is entitled to employ the former in preference to the latter.

Similarly, if a white employer has found that his Negro employees are not satisfactory because of their attitudes toward his supervision, may he not avoid hiring Negroes in the future? Must he turn sociologist and investigate the basis of the connection between being a Negro employee of his and having an unsatisfactory attitude toward his supervision? He might realize that his own personality was partly responsible; but he might also realize that he could not change it with the help available to him. Or he might believe that the attitudes arose because of the earlier experience of his employees with white people. Yet whatever the grounds of his belief in the connection between being a Negro and being unsuitable, the employer, according to this principle of probable indicators, is not practising racially discriminatory hiring. He is not opposed to dark skin but to certain qualities accidentally conjoined with its bearers. If this connection were to be broken for any reason, he would employ Negroes.

However, this view does not seem to differ, in any relevant respect, from that of the employer who says that he believes most American Negroes at the present time to be dishonest, feckless, violent, and that for these reasons he would never hire one if he could avoid doing so. He, too, does not discriminate against Negro applicants merely because of their race. He refuses to hire them because he believes contemporary American Negroes, in general, to have undesirable personal qualities. Perhaps in the future they will not. 'Meanwhile', he says privately, 'I will not employ Negro-applicants. I am not discriminating against them on racial grounds, for I am not giving them unequal treatment "merely because of their minority characteristics". The qualities to which I object are not connected by natural laws with the possession of dark skin. They are simply associated with it at the moment because of unfortunate social conditions. When these change I will change my policy.'

It is but a short slide from this view to that of one kind of acknowledged discriminator. He has only to add the qualifying words, 'But of course those conditions are not likely to change and therefore neither are the undesirable characteristics of Negro employees. It would be better if both were different, but then it would be better if the whole world were different. So we must make do with things as they are. I, for one, am reasonably content with them.' To this we can hardly object that the crucial difference between such a view and the previous one lies simply in a difference of attitude: one man does not, as a matter of policy, employ Negroes at present but wishes they were different so that he could; the other has the same policy but does not have that wish. The difference between a policy of discrimination and a policy of non-discrimination cannot lie merely in the practitioner's satisfaction with it. There are willing discriminators and unwilling ones, willing supporters of fair employment laws and reluctant conformers to them. These obvious distinctions could not be drawn if attitude alone made the vital difference. Nor would it be necessary for a change in policy to be more than a change in wishes. The action taken would remain the same.

On the other hand, the dictionary definition of 'discrimination' offers us no help here. If 'discrimination' is defined as treatment based on the group to which the person belongs rather than on his individual merit, then the definition excludes too much. Every person belongs to an indefinitely large number of classes, since every one of his indefinitely large number of properties determines a corresponding class. And of these classes a similarly large number will be minority classes in the sense that the majority of logically possible members are not actual members. Most men do not in fact belong to the class of twelve-toed men, although it is logically possible that all men should belong to the class. More important still, we can always use some property or set of properties to form a class of which a particular individual is in fact the only member. For example, Napoleon is the only member of the class 'Corsicans who have been Commander-in-Chief of the French army'. Hence, all treatment based on individual merit is also treatment based on a class, since the meritorious properties for which the person is being selected can also be used to determine such a class. The desired contrast between minority class and individual merit vanishes, and with it the hope of picking out discriminators from non-discriminators.

An apparent way round this objection is this. Interpret the term 'minority' as referring only to the characteristics named in a regulation, for example, race, religion, ethnic origin. Then lay it down that treatment justified by inference from these *particular* characteristics to individual merit—where merit is decisive—will be discriminatory. But to adopt this interpretation is to reject the principle of probable indicators as it is applied to the named characteristics. Inferences from race, religion, and ethnic origin to specific, relevant qualities will be forbidden on the ground that the former are commonly not accurate signs of the latter. If they were—if lawlike associations were present—then treatment justified by inference from them need not be discriminatory. Since the associations present are not lawlike, however, they are subject to change, at least in the longer run. Thus they offer no firm basis for a social policy with important consequences. We have, so the argument goes, no assurance that the practical man will adjust his probable indicators to changing conditions; in fact the temporal lag in such adjustments is notoriously large. So while an employer need not turn sociologist in order to account for a particular conjunction of properties, neither is he entitled to rely on it in hiring men. He is entitled to rely, in this field, only on the absence of lawlike associations between race, religion, and ethnic origin on the one hand, and relevant personal qualities on the other.

On this view the Negro employer who refused to hire American Negroes *was* discriminating against them. True, his discrimination was based on his belief that the applicants would feel resentful toward him, and this belief was a major cause—a sufficient condition —of his refusal to hire. But he arrived at this belief by means of an inference from the principle of probable indicators, an inference which is ruled out by the proposed definition of 'discrimination'.

However, we are then faced with the task of framing this definition. We might try, 'treatment not based on individual qualifications alone, where these are decisive, but based at least in part on race, religion, or ethnic origin'. Here the phrase 'based at least in part' will mean 'at least a non-redundant part of one sufficient but unnecessary condition'. That is, race, religion, or ethnic origin are causes in at least the following sense: the three of them form a set; and this set is such that *any* one member of it is necessary to make certain other conditions which are present in a given situation sufficient to produce the effect —the discriminatory treatment.[1] This interpretation will also admit all the stronger cases, those in which the employer's attitudes toward race, religion, or ethnic origin are themselves either necessary or sufficient conditions for the rejection of the applicant. Being a non-redundant part of one sufficient but unnecessary condition is the weakest causal relation admitted here. If the employer's attitudes do

[1] See J. L. Mackie, 'Causes and Conditions', *American Philosophical Quarterly*, 2, October 1965, pp. 245–64.

not meet even this description, they make no causal contribution to the effect. Their absence will make no difference to the treatment actually given.

2. Treatment based on individual qualifications alone

We still have to indicate when individual qualifications alone are to be taken as decisive. It may be reasonable that a Catholic marriage guidance centre be staffed only by Catholic counsellors, but is it also reasonable that Negro suburbs have only Negro policemen? Is there a relevant difference between the two cases? One common answer is that being of a particular race, religion, and ethnic origin is sometimes in itself an essential, and hence non-discriminatory, qualification for the satisfactory performance of certain tasks. A Catholic marriage guidance centre is designed to make help available from Catholic teaching and doctrine, and this aid can be given only by those convinced of its truth, namely Catholics. But suburbs, even Negro ones, are not designed to be policed by Negroes. Nor is it obvious that only they can do this work, since there is nothing in it for which they alone can be trained. Hence the religious qualification is an essential part of the job description, the racial one is not, even though being a Negro policeman may be an accidental advantage in a Negro suburb.

This answer relies on the soundness of the distinction between a qualification which forms an essential and non-discriminatory part of a job description and a qualification which does not. But how is this distinction to be put? An essential qualification cannot be simply one which is necessary to satisfactory performance in the job. Being a Negro may be a necessary condition for satisfactory performance as a policeman in a black ghetto. And being a Catholic believer may not be necessary to a counsellor who is both knowledgeable about Catholicism and sympathetic to its teachings on marriage. If we reply that as a practical matter it is necessary to be a Catholic believer in order to perform satisfactorily as a Catholic counsellor, then the parallel with the case of the Negro policeman becomes even closer. As a temporary experiment we might disguise white policemen as Negroes in order to show that actually being a Negro was not necessary to performing the work, and that what was necessary was being thought to be a Negro. As a permanent arrangement this would hardly do.

Yet once we agree that being a Negro and being a Catholic are both essential, and hence non-discriminatory, requirements for certain jobs, we shall be forced back into supporting the principle of probable indicators. For we shall be claiming that under many sorts of special circumstances we *are* justified in inferring from race, religion, and ethnic origin to the candidates' qualifications. Of course these qualifications may be described only as the absence of certain qualities—racist attitudes, for example. But any property can be described as the absence of its complement, so this will be no point of distinction. Nor can we argue that we are not really invoking the principle, that we are not making the proscribed inference from race, religion, or ethnic origin to independent personal qualities since we are inferring from the former merely to some of the defining properties which compose them. For instance, we can infer from the fact that John is a Roman Catholic that he will believe that the Church is the 'infallible interpreter of revealed truth'; this follows as a matter of definition.

However, most of our inferences to candidates' qualifications will not be of this kind. Most of our inferences obviously will invoke the principle of probable indicators. Some of them will be conclusions drawn about the responses of other people to the candidate's race, religion, or ethnic origin, and of his reaction to their responses. Thus we may conclude that a Negro applicant for the job of school teacher will be less frightening to young Negro children than will a white teacher, and therefore that the Negro's responses to the children will be less harsh. Again, some of our inferences will be straightforward conclusions about the personal properties associated with being a member of a particular race or religion under given local conditions; the high educational aspirations of Japanese-Americans is an example.

On the other hand, if we agree that, in our two cases, being a Negro and being a Catholic are *not* essential requirements, under what conditions, if any, will they be? No doubt it is necessary to be a Catholic in order to be eligible for the Catholic priesthood. It is also essential to be a member of the Ku Klux Klan in order to be employed as Grand Dragon. The two organizations differ in that Catholicism is open to people of all races and ethnic backgrounds whereas the Ku Klux Klan is not. They agree in demanding certain religious qualifications. In contrast, a Negro dance ensemble has no religious requirements but employs only Negroes. Why should we say, then, that the Klan discriminates against Negroes, Catholics, and Jews, but that the Roman Church and the dance company discriminate against no one? All three organizations necessarily exclude from membership some racial or religious groups, and the exclusion is required by the goals which these organizations pursue. But if some instances of exclusion by definition are discriminatory and some are not, what accounts for the difference? It cannot be merely that some organizational goals incorporate certain discriminatory practices and some goals do not. For while this is true, since Klansmen want to eliminate Catholic power, but Negro dancers do not want to suppress their white colleagues, nothing new follows from this distinction.

The reason why nothing new follows is that an exclusion is supposed to be discriminatory if the organizational goal to which it is a means is discriminatory. Yet our test of discrimination is the same in both cases—exclusion from membership and exclusion by goal—namely, 'admission based at least in part on race, religion, or ethnic origin'. So the test will give the same answer in both cases: what this answer is in any given instance will depend on how we characterize the organizational goals. Thus the sole result of introducing their characterization into the debate is to recapitulate all the previous argument. If the Catholic heaven and the Moslem paradise are goals open only to true believers, then, by this goal-oriented test, employment limited to Catholics and Muslims discriminates against Protestants and Jews. Again, employment limited to Negro dancers discriminates against non-Negroes if the goal of these dancers is simply to have a successful Negro dance company. If it is later to have a company in which non-Negroes may dance, then present exclusionary practices cannot be required by *that* goal. Hence, in arguing that the essential requirements for a job are those prescribed by the goals of the organization we are not finding a new way of answering the question 'Are these requirements discriminatory?' We are simply changing the question to 'Are those goals discriminatory?', and then giving the same answer as before, although in practice the second question may be easier to answer than the first.

3. Rejecting the principle of probable indicators

The upshot of our discussion so far is this. If we accept the legitimacy of the principle of probable indicators we force ourselves to accept as non-discriminatory some actions which we should prefer to classify as discriminatory. If we reject the principle, we seem not to be able to determine, by any straightforward means, when individual qualifications alone are to be taken as decisive or essential, and thus apparently cannot frame a useful definition of 'discrimination'. Nor can we easily go on to answer the question whether equivalence of training and performance is a sufficient test of discrimination, a test which might well be referred to by that definition. How, then, are we to release ourselves from this deadlock?

One way is to retrace some of our steps. The various definitions of 'discrimination' all embody the view that the discriminator acts upon a false belief: he believes that, as things now stand, he can, in general, reliably infer from a person's race, religion, or ethnic background to his personal qualifications. Moreover, the implication is that not only are such inferences unreliable in fact but that we must, as a matter of social policy, do everything possible to ensure that they remain unreliable. And the best way of ensuring this is to prevent them from ever being made. For every time such an inference is correct it increases, by imposition of the majority's stereotype on the minority, the likelihood that the next inference will be reliable. Oppressed minorities eventually display the qualities attributed to them by their oppressors. This chain of self-strengthening inferences must be broken from the outside, since a person actually engaged in making them believes that he gains more by doing so than by abstaining.

Thus given the social importance of eliminating discriminatory practices, the cost of the consistent rejection of the principle of probable indicators will have to be accepted. We shall have to agree that individual qualifications are always to be taken as decisive, and that racial, religious, and ethnic affiliations are never to count as essential conditions of employment. Our definition of 'discriminatory employment' will then read, 'differential treatment not based on a difference of individual qualifications alone, but based at least in part on race, religion, or ethnic origin'. Under this definition, equivalence of training and performance will be a sufficient test for the discovery of discrimination, and our definition can easily be reworded to include this information. The final definition will be: 'differential treatment not based on a difference of individual qualifications, e.g. training and performance, alone, but based at least in part on race, religion, or ethnic origin'. The phrase 'based at least in part' will have to be interpreted in the manner previously described—as a non-redundant part of one sufficient but unnecessary condition. It logically follows from this definition that differential treatment where individual qualifications are equivalent is discriminatory.

If we are willing to accept, for reasons of general social policy, a definition as strong as this, we shall label as discriminatory the practices of our various employers who refused to hire Negroes because of their supposed attitudes or behaviour toward white supervisors in general. We shall have to say that the apparent jealousy, dishonesty, and violence of these employees must be put up with for the greater good of the broader policy; and that we believe that the continued operation of non-discriminatory hiring over a period of time will eliminate some of the conditions which produce these undesirable characteristics. Finally, we shall have to remember that we have limited the use of the principle of probable indicators by decree. As new forms of discrimination arise we shall have to extend our writ to deal with them, for example, in the case of qualified women not given employment because of their sex.

The practical difficulties of adopting so strong a definition of 'discriminatory employment' are obvious. We force employers to take on applicants who are thought to have undesirable qualities, and not to hire applicants less well qualified but otherwise better liked; we forbid many useful arrangements like that of staffing Negro districts exclusively with Negro teachers and policemen, and we make the hiring procedures of churches, religious societies and ethnic clubs rather complicated and unnatural.

However, there are equally obvious advantages. The chief one is that we do not allow potential discriminators to trade on certain ambiguities in the use of such phrases as 'racially discriminatory'. Thus when a person says that he dislikes and discriminates against Negroes he sometimes claims that his attitude is a response to their physical characteristics alone. He is repelled by their darker skin, their short kinky hair, their platyrrhine noses. At other times the discriminator says that his attitude is a reaction to certain additional qualities which he believes all or most people with those physical characteristics to have. He may think that there is a law-like association between possessing those physical features and possessing these additional qualities. Or he may think that the connection is accidental but relatively stable. At still other times the discriminator may suggest that he is repelled by both the physical qualities and their associated ones.

Now the reluctant employers whom we earlier described claim not to practise discriminatory hiring. They deny holding any of these views except that of there being an accidental connection between racial affiliation and undesired qualities. For this reason they claim not to be discriminating against Negro applicants because of their 'minority characteristics'. But, clearly, the important question is, 'What characteristics are these? The physical ones? Or those thought to be associated with them in some law-like fashion?' By choosing the first alternative, some employers, though not those we have described, may claim to be free of discrimination. Yet it is more than doubtful whether anyone has ever tried to give a rational defence of a discriminatory social practice merely by appealing to the physical features of the rejected group. Tastes of this sort are often used in the selection of friends; but how could a dislike of curly hair or of a particular physical type be given as a relevant reason for refusing employment to its possessor? Even the most confirmed racist does not argue that as a matter of public policy Negroes should be discriminated against *simply* because they have identifiable Negro ancestors. His argument is that a certain kind of ancestry has a law-like connection with certain disqualifying characteristics. And the racist's enthusiasm for ferreting out this ancestry reveals his belief that physical appearances alone may be deceptive. The fatal connection is thought to be between an invisible biological structure, like the gene, and the disqualifying personal qualities. A Negro who can pass as a white person will nevertheless display those same qualities. Black skin is only a convenient, though not a necessary, means of identification.

However, our examples of reluctant employers have been drawn from a rather different group. These employers claim to have rejected the racist's belief in a law-like connection and to have substituted a belief in an accidental connection. Might not the belief they substitute be correct? Suppose our Negro employer was correct in thinking that most of his Negro applicants would be resentful. Would he then not have a good reason for refusing to employ them? In order to give a useful answer to this question we must assume that the employer was not correct solely by accident. He must have arrived at his belief by a reputable procedure, one that allows for counter-argument and an appropriate response to it. In that case he will be committed to revising his belief as circumstances change. But if his only general guide is the principle of probable indicators that continual process of revision cannot take place. For since the association of properties on which he relies is not based on laws, it may change at any time because of changes in the social conditions which have produced the association. By hypothesis the employer has no independent information about these relevant social changes; and if he had there would be no need for him to rely, even in part, on the principle of probable indicators. He could rely directly on the causative social conditions themselves for knowledge about the likely attitudes of his applicants. Therefore the employer, by his refusal constantly to sample new applicants, cuts himself off from all possibility of learning about changes in the rule of association by which he is guided. His particular employment of the principle of probable indicators will be self-confirming, since no counter-examples can ever gain entry.

Thus the principle of probable indicators cannot be satisfactory by itself as a procedural rule. On the other hand, when it is taken in conjunction with more adequate information about causal factors, it becomes superfluous. True, our use of the principle may give correct results on specific occasions. But this will be due to luck and not to any knowledge about the soundness of the principle's applicability on those occasions. Not only does social gambling of this type give poor returns while yet entrenching itself as an appropriate method, it also makes replacement by a more satisfactory rule very difficult. These are ample reasons for bringing the appeal to accidental connections—and thus the reliance on the principle of probable indicators—under the heading 'discriminatory practice'. From the cost of adopting such a strong definition of 'discrimination' must be subtracted the considerable expense of using a procedural rule which is certain to produce some false beliefs in its employers.

4. Discriminators and discriminatory practices

One of our earlier questions was this: 'Can equivalence of qualifications (training and performance) be used as a practical and sufficient test for the presence of undiscriminatory hiring? Is it a test to which a useful definition of such hiring might well refer us?' Our answer has been that the strong definition, or criterion of application, we have given of 'discriminatory employment' ('differential treatment not based on a difference of individual qualifications, e.g. training and performance, alone, but based at least in part on race, religion, or ethnic origin') will have this test as one of its logical consequences. The definition excludes all factors but individual qualification, so the test must be sufficient. And we have already given reasons for thinking that it is practical: namely, that an employer must know what he counts as equivalent qualifications, and that there are various ways of discovering, either with or without his co-operation, whether he has taken account of qualifications alone.

There is, however, a further question about the wording of our definition. Why, if only individual qualifications matter, do we need to refer to race, religion, or ethnic group? By eliminating these references we can also eliminate the need to extend the definition when new forms of discriminatory hiring appear. They will be excluded as effectively by the shortened version of the definition as by an extended definition. Why itemize them when there is no reason to do so?

This question neglects an important point. It is that our definition is of 'discriminatory employment' and not of 'discrimination'. We have only excluded certain itemized uses of the principle of probable indicators and not its use in general. We have, in brief, not tried to give a general definition of 'discriminatory behaviour'—a rule for recognizing such behaviour in all its possible varieties. And one reason for not doing so is that only certain forms of discriminatory behaviour fall within the domain of public interest. These are not the only forms which sociologists wish to define and measure; but it is only inferences concerning these forms of discrimination, inferences drawn with the aid of the principle of probable indicators, which are proscribed by our definition. If a man refuses, on principle, to have Jews as guests in his home, the principle may be contemptible. Yet his actions cannot be described as a 'treatment not based on individual qualifications alone'. For there are no qualifications which any social institution can lay down concerning one person's admission as a desired guest into another man's home. A host is free to consult his own taste.

It is pointless, then, for social scientists either to try to give a *general* operational procedure for applying the term 'discrimination', or to worry, as social scientists, about all the *private* errors into which we can be led by discriminatory inferences. It is pointless because of the difficulty, discussed earlier, of making a general distinction between individual qualifications and qualifications based on group or class membership. Because of this difficulty we are forced to specify the classes whose members are discriminated against; and we could not possibly specify by any one procedure the indefinitely large number of all such classes. Private forms of discrimination are endless in type, since every individual person, every club and association, discriminates against many classes of persons—if 'discriminates' simply means 'making a distinction in favour of or against, a person or thing based on the group, class, or category to which that person or thing belongs rather than on individual merit'. Social scientists may, of course, study various forms of private discrimination, but the definitions they use must reflect the fact that the discrimination concerned is a matter of private taste and judgment and not a matter for public policy. Discriminatory housing, employment, and education are practices of great public concern. The exclusion of Jews, Catholics, Negroes, homosexuals, and communists from certain clubs is often not. It becomes so only when the internal affairs of such clubs affect the larger society in some important way, as when they become centres for political cabals.

The reason, then, why our criterion of application of the term 'discriminatory employment' must specifically exclude race, religion, and ethnic origin as individual qualifications is clear. We have no other way of ensuring that these factors, and others yet to come, will not be counted as types of qualification. This is especially obvious in the preference given to minority political candidates in their own minority districts, or in arrangements for proportional representation of each ethnic group within a municipal area. The addition of the phrase, 'training and performance alone', is not sufficient to prevent these practices, since they are commonly defended by the claim that a particular affiliation is either necessary or advantageous in achieving the required performance. The only general way to eliminate this defence is to forbid reliance on racial, religious, or ethnic group membership as a qualification for employment.

Hence both discrimination and prejudice have this feature in common: both incorporate the notion of a judgment supported by an unreliable type of inference, and thus supported by irrelevant reasons. Discrimination is the putting into practice of such judgments; if, in addition, they are resistant to change by rational argument, we are entitled to call them 'prejudices'. But whether or not they are also prejudices, these judgments may be put into practice by someone who does not himself adhere to them. A kind-hearted slave salesman makes a living by the practice of discrimination on behalf of his clients. Because such people may be agents for discriminators without themselves being practitioners on principle, it is worth while to note that our definition is of discriminatory *employment*. But by itself this definition will not enable us to locate and recognize employers who are practitioners on principle. Our definition helps to answer the question 'Is discriminatory employment present here?' and not 'Is there a committed discriminator present here?'

Now if we did wish to answer this latter question we should first have to be clear about the sense of the expression, 'committed discriminatory employer'. And in order to become clear about that sense we should have to consider cases of this sort: suppose that a liberal American business man employs Negroes in his Northern offices but excludes them from his Southern offices whenever his clients object— on the sole ground that overriding the wishes of white clients is bad for profits. Suppose he is correct and that Negro employees do drive away white clients; suppose also that he is not violating the law. Is he practising discrimination though not himself a discriminator? Or is he merely condoning the practices of true discriminators while not himself being a full-fledged practitioner?

This business man does not himself hold a principle which embodies racial discrimination, but he does hold dear the principle of making a good living from his business. This principle, he knows, will lead him to be an unwilling agent for those who wish to see discriminatory hiring enforced. Let us assume that the business man acquiesces in a practice which he believes to be morally wrong. Then he not only permits (does not prevent) discriminatory hiring in his offices, but he enforces it. He does not merely overlook or condone discrimination, he practises it, though unwillingly and against his moral principle. So by the force of his circumstances he is committed to the practice of discrimination, yet he is not committed by principle. He is a practitioner rather than a mere condoner, but he is not a full-fledged practitioner.

By examining cases such as this we might be able to distinguish in a useful way between mere condoners of discrimination and varieties of practitioners. However, the more important point is this. In assigning different degrees of responsibility to people, we require information about their intentions and motives which we do not need if we wish simply to locate the existence of discriminatory practices. It is not the definition of '*discriminatory practice*' which requires us to make some causal inference to the agent's intentions and motives, for we can discriminate without intending to do so and without having any goal in mind. It is the definitions of various sorts of *discriminators* which require us to have knowledge about the agents' thoughts and desires. Hence, we should not compound our difficulties, as Blalock has done, by thinking that the two different problems both demand the same sort of concealed information about people's private attitudes.

We began this long discussion of discrimination with Blalock's view that definitions of discriminatory behaviour are faulty. They do not help us, he said, either to locate or to measure cases of the 'unequal treatment of equals', since the definitions give us no practical means of determining whether the unequal treatment is due to minority characteristics or to some other factor. We have tried to meet this objection by arguing, first, that the supposed difficulty of measurement can be surmounted by direct methods and, second, that our revised definition does provide a practical and sufficient test. If this argument is correct, it becomes obvious why we cannot and should not wish to do away with the notion of discrimination in favour of various measures of inequality. The reason is not, as Blalock suggests, that the notion of discrimination is convenient to use. It is that we are concerned, in this problem, with the inequalities produced by a certain class of agents—by discriminators. If there were no such agents there would be no such inequalities, though there would be inequalities caused by other factors. To eliminate the notion of discrimination would be to eliminate the notion of discriminators. And not to think of them would be to make mysterious the inequalities which they produce. But thinking clearly about the causal source of these inequalities was one of the chief problems with which we were supposed to cope. Nothing was said about changing this problem.

Of course someone might reply that what is important is finding out why discriminators discriminate in specific ways. What factors influence such people to behave as they do—discriminatingly? The notion of discrimination is convenient, he might add, because it intervenes between these more basic causal factors and the resultant social inequalities. Yet it is these basic factors which chiefly interest us, not the trivial truth that discriminatory practices are carried on by discriminatory people. However, this reply, while otherwise correct, overlooks the difference between explaining why the behaviour of discriminatory people has certain social consequences (inequalities) and explaining why such people behave in this way. It is the behaviour of human agents which produces these inequalities, whatever the factors which produce that behaviour. At least some of these inequalities simply *consist* in a certain sort of behaviour by discriminators, and there is no way in which these discriminators can be eliminated from the explanation of the origin and persistence of these inequalities. What could replace the agents? Certainly not the more basic factors, whichever ones they might be. They influence the agents, and only through them influence the inequalities that the agents produce. For this reason we cannot skip over discriminators in the causal process as though they are dispensable—as though we might choose to do without them in accounting for our figures of social inequalities.

5. Discrimination as an implicitly relational term

We can now return to the problems from which we started. One of those problems was why sociologists have difficulty in defining certain terms in such a way that they can be used to refer to measurable properties of theoretical interest. Our example of 'discrimination', or 'discriminatory hiring', can make a contribution toward answering this question. For the example shows us how our adoption of a particular definition, or operational specification, of 'discrimination' is the outcome of a policy judgment. One social policy differs from another in the judgments of this sort which it incorporates. In each case what counts as a discriminatory practice will be determined by the social or legal standard which is incorporated in the chosen policy.

Similar considerations hold for many other terms of social science: amongst them are 'prejudice', 'delinquent', 'social deviant', 'aliena-tion', 'undue deference', 'unsuccessful rehabilitation', 'criminal behaviour', and 'relative deprivation'. These terms form a class whose distinguishing feature is that they embody the notion of observable divergence from an appropriate social or public standard for the kind of behaviour in question. A delinquent is someone who offends against some rule or law; a prejudice is a refusal to be guided by rational argument; a person in a state of relative deprivation believes that there is an unjust difference between the standard benefits to which any person in his situation is entitled and those lesser ones which he is actually receiving. Each such divergence is, in principle, observable. It is the sociologist's task to find out whether such divergences are also measurable in practice—for they will not be if the standard is vague—and if so by what means. But in order to do this he must be quite clear that he is trying to measure devia-tions from a given social standard, or in practical terms, trying to measure dispersion from a group mean. Since different communities, groups, and societies rely on different standards for the same kind of behaviour, what the sociologist will be trying to measure under the same heading—'discriminatory employment' for example—will vary greatly at different times and places.

The reason, then, why it is not merely difficult but impossible to give one acceptable operational specification for each term of this class is that such terms are *implicitly relational*. Their dictionary definitions give us, and can give us, only a general characterization of the kinds of relations to which the terms refer. It is impossible in practice for these definitions to provide us with the information sufficient for recognizing an instance of the relations to which they refer: that is, to be operational specifications. For that information must be composed of two ingredients, neither of which can be described, in all its variations, by the dictionary, or general definition. One ingredient is the end or goal or purpose for which the social standard in question is present. For example, different laws against the same form of discrimination have different aims and purposes. The other ingredient is the particular, and varying, set of features or properties which form the content of the social standard. This set of properties alters with changes in purposes, of course, and hence the different aims of different communities are reflected in the varying content of their social standards, and thus of the terms used to describe those standards.

Now, clearly, there is no reason for a sociologist to complain about the operational usefulness of a dictionary definition of an implicitly relational term unless he has some scientific or practical purpose in studying the relations to which the term refers. One such *practical* purpose is that of implementing an egalitarian social policy. To execute such a policy he must know the extent of the discrimination which it seeks to remove; and to obtain this knowledge he must first undertake a critical examination of the kinds of discriminatory practices which he would like the definition to prohibit. Our extended discussion of a practical and sufficient test for discriminatory employment was an example of this kind. But if we attempt to define an implicitly relational term like 'discriminatory employment' in a sociologically useful fashion—so that we can recognize instances—we shall be forced to specify both the aim and content of the particular standard we employ, whether it be that of the investigator or that of the group which he studies. In doing so we shall be acknowledging that our specification has been adopted as a judgment of someone's social policy; that we can no more define, and hence measure, discrimination *per se* than we can define and measure small, large or heavy things *per se*. Recognizing a horse as small requires a different standard from recognizing a child as small: even a small child knows that a small horse would be a very large child. Because our ordinary concepts of discrimination and discriminatory employment are implicitly relational, they do not become determinate, operational concepts until we specify some particular social policy.

Attempts to circumvent the relational feature of the class of terms to which 'discrimination' belongs are pointless. For not only is it impossible in practice to give a *general* characterization (a single operational specification) of all the different aims and contents of the many different social standards to which a term like 'discrimination' can refer, but there is no good reason why we should want to do so. Such a monolithic characterization (or general definition) of 'discrimination', for instance, can amount only to saying that discrimination is the putting into practice of judgments about people that are not based on the relevant qualifications of those people. But there is no theory or practical consideration which would enable us to use such a non-operational definition for any specifically sociological purpose. We require operational criteria, and these must specify the particular policy standard being used. Once we realize that what counts as discriminatory behaviour has to be *decided upon* as a matter of social policy, the desire to define and measure discriminatory behaviour, or even discriminatory employment, in general, disappears, and with it the wish to have a *single* operational specification of 'discrimination' or of 'discriminatory employment'.

Moreover, in so far as the critics' original demand for 'measurable properties of theoretical interest' refers to implicitly relational terms, the demand is misguided. A property of theoretical interest is one which plays an essential part in some theory. The extent of the property's theoretical interest will depend on how successful and far-ranging the theory is, and on how central a position the property occupies in it. So a demand for 'measurable properties of theoretical interest' is, in fact, a demand for successful theories about measurable properties. To argue that human social life has no properties of the required sort is to argue that no successful theories about measurable properties are possible.

But this conclusion cannot be established by taking implicitly relational terms as the names of properties of theoretical interest, properties which form a reasonable test of the sociologists' performance. Such terms, if the preceding argument is correct, do not offer a reasonable test. They offer no test at all, since they are not, as they stand, the names of measurable properties. The names are incomplete, since the relations referred to by terms like 'discrimination', 'discriminatory employment', 'delinquency', and 'social deviance' rely, in each case, on an implicit and unspecified social standard. Until this is specified, divergence from it cannot be observed or measured. Once it is specified, it can be used to test for the presence of the property; and different standards will produce different results in the case of the same term. This shows us that the mere dictionary definitions of these terms as they stand do not direct us to what is to be observed or measured. Because their definitions do not so direct us, the terms by themselves are not the names of *measurable* properties. Hence they are not appropriate candidates for the title 'measurable properties of theoretical interest'. It is not that implicitly relational terms have been tried and found wanting by critics of sociology, and thus provide good evidence against the existence of the desired properties. Rather, such terms are not eligible for the trial, for it is logically impossible that they should meet the requirements of eligibility.

We have been arguing that in sociology there is a large set of important terms which are implicitly relational; and that while such terms become applicable only as a result of particular policy decisions —as a result of specifying particular social standards—this fact often goes unrecognized. Its significance for the development of social laws will be discussed later in chapter six, section 2. At present it is worth mentioning this much. The difference between 'discriminatory hiring' and 'discriminatory hiring of Negroes because of their race' is that between an expression referring to a *relation* (discriminatory hiring) and an expression referring to a *relational property* (the property of discriminating in employment against Negroes). Discriminatory hiring of Catholics is a different relational property from that of discriminating in employment against Negroes. But these two properties of the discriminator exemplify the same relation—that of discriminatory hiring—which holds between the discriminator and his various kinds of victims.

Now discriminatory hiring, like its genus, discriminatory treatment, is a tetradic relation: there is the practitioner, the victim, the respect in which the discriminatory treatment is practised, and the grounds on which it is based. Thus Jones behaves (un)favourably towards Barnes with respect to employment because of Barnes' race. When we recognize an instance of such (un)favourable treatment we are in possession of all four terms of the relation. We are able to attribute a relational property to a particular agent, Jones, because a particular social standard enables us to recognize a practice as discriminatory; and we recognize a practice as discriminatory because of the grounds on which it is based. In specifying such a standard, then, we equip ourselves with a criterion for recognizing exemplifications of a relation: that is, for picking out certain relational properties. The difference between a general definition of 'discriminatory hiring' and a sociologically useful one is the difference between the lexical definition of a relation-term and the stipulative definition of a relational-property expression. Until we stipulate, by adoption of a particular policy, what is to count as an exemplification of the relation 'discriminatory hiring', the mere lexical definition will not serve the needs of either social investigators or legislators. For if we cannot recognize the exemplifications of such policy-dependent relations as 'discrimination', 'prejudice', and 'delinquent', we can neither legislate about these forms of behaviour nor study them. In particular, we cannot be clear as to the distinction between trying to find a social law which refers to policy-dependent relations and trying to find a social law which refers to their exemplifications—to relational properties. It is by no means obvious that the two sorts of attempt will be equally useful.

Once we have come to appreciate the prevalence of policy-dependent terms in sociology, there still remains the serious problem of how we can produce definitions of measurable properties of theoretical interest. It is of some help to realize that covertly relational terms must *not* be taken as the names of either relational properties or qualities. But what *must* we do?

At first glance, it is by no means clear that a satisfactory answer can be given to this question, for its phrasing may suggest that we should be searching for a technique which would help us to produce such definitions. But if we eliminate this suggestion on the ground that there *can be* no technique for the production of successful definitions, we are left with more sober alternatives. These include whatever hints and tips we can gather from the efforts which sociologists have made to discover properties of theoretical significance. Whether or not these efforts have been successful, it is still most important for us to consider them. They represent the best evidence we have as to the feasibility of using present sociological methods for the definition and measurement of significant properties. The actual successes, or failures, of these methods are less interesting, for our purposes, than are the reasons why they have succeeded—or failed.

Properties

Chapter three

1. The multidimensionality of prejudice and authoritarianism

Earlier it was suggested that complaints about the uselessness of certain sociological definitions arise from the demand, reasonable on its face, that sociologists produce definitions which refer to measurable properties of theoretical interest. However, it is clear that the only satisfactory answer to this demand is the *discovery* of such properties. No mere tinkering of the definitions of terms will enable us to give them a theoretical point; that will have to be supplied by the work they do in theories. Hence the production of these theories and the discovery of such properties will go hand in hand. But while the property terms of a theory are often pointless when stripped from it, nothing requires us to assume that the theory itself is coherent or that its other terms are adequate. The search for the desired properties may fail in a variety of ways and for a number of different reasons. Our immediate task, then, is to note what sociologists have already produced; and our subsequent task is to say what this shows us about the procedures used and how these procedures bear on future prospects for the discovery of desirable properties.

It is convenient and, more than that, enlightening to turn again to the topic of prejudice, and in particular to some problems discussed by Blalock under the heading 'Social Psychological Studies of Prejudice'.[1] He there describes some work on 'attitudinal variables'. These are personality features as classified by, and tested in, certain questionnaires. The attitudinal variables include, says Blalock, 'factors such as anxiety, frustration, authoritarianism, rigidity, alienation, status concern, conservatism, and conventionalism'.[2] These factors are thought by some investigators, at least, to be

[1] *Toward a Theory of Minority-Group Relations*, New York, 1967, pp. 2–10.
[2] *Ibid.*, p. 2.

41

correlated in some causal fashion with the presence of prejudiced opinions. Blalock's question, then, is whether such a causal connection exists. Does any person who displays 'unsubstantiated, firmly held, prejudgments of individuals and groups' also display certain other personality features? And if so, do some of these features cause (in some sense of 'cause') the person to hold prejudgments of that sort?

Now the difficulty to which Blalock first turns his attention is that of the high intercorrelation amongst these other personality features, and thus to the difficulty of determining their individual relationship to prejudice. More fundamental, however, is the problem which he refers to as 'multidimensionality of scales': that is, inaccuracy of tests due to their eliciting information about a set of loosely related, or in some cases independent, personality features rather than the desired information about one feature alone. He calls this 'the proliferation of dimensions', and says in the case of authoritarianism, for example, that if it is true that the F-scale actually elicits seven different dimensions, the correlating of each of these with prejudice will be required. And if it is also true that prejudice itself has three dimensions, then, Blalock says, 'twenty-one relationships must be studied, rather than the single one between authoritarianism and prejudice.'[1] Thus, we shall have to find out which of these twenty-one relationships are worth studying.

Clearly, we need to take a closer look at this 'proliferation of dimensions', for it is a process which may begin again with the introduction of each new variable. What, then, are we claiming when we state, as Blalock does, that 'prejudice itself is not unidimensional, that one may readily distinguish between cognitive, emotional and evaluative dimensions of prejudice'?[2] When we turn to the author[3] on whom Blalock is relying for this distinction, we find the following account of these three 'dimensions'.

The *cognitive dimension* concerns 'the question of how the individual perceives the group—what he believes about the group'.[4] Also included is 'cognitive orientation'. This latter consists in certain features which belong to the person's beliefs about minority groups. One example is the tendency to think of people only in terms of their group membership. Another example is the importance of such a belief to the believer. A third example is his recognition, as expressed in his beliefs, of the existence of 'minority problems'. Leaving aside those features which fall under 'cognitive orientation', the remainder

---

[1] *Ibid.*, p. 7.
[2] *Ibid.*
[3] B. M. Kramer in 'Dimensions of Prejudice', *Journal of Psychology*, 27, April 1949, pp. 389–451.
[4] *Ibid.*, p. 394.

of the *cognitive dimension* consists in 'what the person believes about the group'. Instances of such beliefs are: the group's intellectual and biological inferiority, their unrestrained gratification of impulses, and their clannishness.

The second (or emotional) *dimension* concerns the emotional attitudes held toward the group: fear, distrust, disgust, contempt and envy are examples. The third (or *action*, not evaluative) *dimension* refers to the person's tendencies to action as inferred from his verbal responses. These tendencies include: rejection in direct personal relations like marriage and friendship; rejection for close personal relations like those in clubs and sporting activities; rejection of residential proximity; enforcement of economic and political inequality; physical aggression.

So much for the complications thought to attach to the notion, and practice, of prejudice. Let us now take a brief look at the issues raised by the notion of the authoritarian personality. We can then bring together the two sets of issues and thus consider the force of Blalock's complaint about the 'proliferation of dimensions' and the ensuing 'multiplicity of scales'.

The 'authoritarian personality' is a phrase which refers to people 'with a history of strict treatment in childhood and subjection to great social pressure toward conformity'. They 'are characterized as tending to be rigid and intolerant of ambiguity as adults. They perceive the world as a constant source of threat and tend to identify with conventional values for security . . . these individuals are also ethnocentric and characteristically project their aggressive tendencies on to outgroups . . .'[1]

Now Blalock's criticism of the notion of the authoritarian personality, as measured by the F-scale (the California Public Opinion Scale), is roughly this: the F-scale does not measure all and only the defining properties of the authoritarian personality. The reason why the F-scale does not do so is that it contains both irrelevant questions and questions which cluster undesirably into sub-groups. The presence of these clusters is evidence that the F-scale tests for a number of different features which have been thrown together under the label 'authoritarian personality'. The sources on which Blalock apparently relies for these claims are two papers: one by Christie and Garcia entitled 'Subcultural Variation in Authoritarian Personality', and another by S. F. Camilleri entitled 'A Factor Analysis of the F-Scale'.[2]

According to the former paper, two samples drawn from university students in two different cities produced answers which by correlation

---

[1] R. Christie and J. Garcia, 'Subcultural Variation in Authoritarian Personality', *Journal of Abnormal and Social Psychology*, 46, 1951, pp. 457–69.
[2] *Social Forces*, 37, May 1959, pp. 316–23.

techniques were sub-dividable into clusters. The members of each such cluster were those items (kinds of answers) that correlated more highly with each other than with items outside that cluster. The number of items in the various clusters ranged between two and five; the number of clusters was seven for one city and eight for the other. Each cluster was then given a label which was thought by independent judges to characterize the variable elicited by that cluster. Some instances of these labels were: 'Submission to authority', 'Low opinion of human nature', 'Punitive attitude'. Examples of items falling under the first label—'Submission to authority'—were these two: 'Young people sometimes get rebellious ideas, but as they grow up they ought to get over them and settle down'; 'Some day it will probably be shown that astrology can explain a lot of things'.

Two important facts emerged from this study. First, the two cities had only three clusters with the same label in common. Second, even these three clusters did not include all the same items; the two cities shared these labels in common but did not share all the items falling under those labels. To take the extreme case, 'Submission to authority' was a label under which fell completely different items in the two clusters with that same label. What produced this result was simply that a set of answers given by one group of people in one city was thought by the investigators to be similar enough in its causal origin to be given the same label as a different set of answers given by another group in the other city. This shows, says Blalock, and presumably he is correct, that while the F-scale consistently indicates that there is a close relationship between something called 'the authoritarian personality' and the holding of prejudiced beliefs, it is not at all clear what factors or variables or elements make up that personality. If the two groups shared only three labels (characterizations of factors) out of eight, and those three were not even derived from all the same kinds of answers, we are thrown back upon the investigators' judgments as to the appropriateness of their labels— most of which the two groups did not share. So, at best, the F-scale must be a rag-bag of questions, some of which are proper tests for authoritarianism as defined by the originators of that notion, and some of which may be tests for variables to which Christie and Garcia have applied certain labels. The accuracy of these labels is certainly open to question.

S. F. Camilleri's study[1] provides additional evidence that the F-scale does not measure a single factor—the authoritarian personality—which accounts for all the variations in the respondents' scores. For that personality type is supposed to consist in three basic features: externalized super-ego, as shown, for example, in conventionalism and authoritarian submission; ego weakness, as in

[1] *Op. cit.*

44

superstitiousness and toughness; projection, as in cynicism and destructiveness. But Camilleri's analysis showed that the components of each of these basic features do not correlate together more highly than with the components of the other two features. So the responses obtained from the use of the F-scale do not support the view that there are three basic features of the authoritarian personality. Nor does factor analysis support the claim that these three features form *one* measurable factor, namely, the authoritarian personality. Instead, the variations in F-scale scores can only be explained by assuming that *seven* factors (or traits) are present. This is to say that the F-scale does not test for one factor made up of three basic features, but for seven unknown factors. Thus Camilleri's results are similar to the seven or eight clusters obtained by Christie and Garcia's study.

To refer, then, to a 'proliferation of dimensions' in connection with authoritarianism is to refer to the failure to establish it as a natural kind or complex property. Being authoritarian was supposed to be a uniform association of certain attributes: among them, authoritarian submission, destructiveness and cynicism, authoritarian aggression, superstition and stereotypy, for example. This set of personality features was thought to form a statistically correlated cluster. To argue that these features do not in fact correlate statistically is to argue that no such complex property or natural kind has been shown to exist. If this argument is correct, there is no one attitudinal variable called 'the authoritarian personality' and hence no possible causal connection between it and prejudice. Thus we are returned to Blalock's description of the problem: if we try to measure each of the attributes separately on a unidimensional scale, and are successful in doing so, we shall be left with a series of attitudinal variables. Some of these, at least, are likely to be correlated with prejudice. They will be additions to the lengthy list of such variables already known to be correlated with prejudice. Which of them contributes to prejudice significantly enough to be worth further study?

2. Kramer's three dimensions of prejudice

Clearly, this question should not be considered until we have examined Kramer's view that the word 'prejudice' refers to three dimensions (cognitive, emotional, action), each of which is an independently measurable variable. For even if 'prejudice' is the name of a complex property or natural kind consisting in these three variables, it is not obvious that they are, or can be, three complex *properties* which are capable of causally interacting either with each other or with other attitudinal variables. But if they cannot do this *in practice*, then whatever their utility in the analysis of the concept of prejudice, they are not relevant here. Our problem is that of the causal connection, direct or indirect, between prejudice and its constituent properties on the one hand, and the authoritarian personality and its constituent properties on the other. We wish to know whether the cognitive, emotional, and action dimensions of prejudices are, or are capable of being, three complex properties. It is an independent question whether, if they are, they are uniformly associated with each other so as to form the still more complex property named 'prejudice'.

Now consider some of the undesirable features of Kramer's classification. The 'cognitive dimension' has two parts. One concerns the content of the prejudiced person's beliefs about the people toward whom his prejudice is directed: he believes, for example, that they are dirty and clannish. The other part concerns something quite different. It concerns a miscellaneous set of properties which hold of all prejudiced beliefs: for instance, that they are over-generalizations or that they are important to the believer. But it is perfectly clear that any device which tests for the content of a belief is testing for something distinct from one that tests for the importance of the belief to its possessor; and one that tests for over-generalization, or running beyond the evidence available to the believer, is different from both the other two. *What* is believed is distinct from how *well justified* the believer is in holding that belief, and distinct, also, from how *important* the belief is to the believer.

So here under the label 'cognitive dimension' we have items which may require three different tests. For if our tests are to measure prejudiced beliefs, they must give a measure not only of the number and scope of the subject's beliefs, but also the intensity, or perhaps tenacity, with which they are held. (The intensity and tenacity are often but not always co-extensive: a man can hold a belief with fervour but drop it as soon as he learns of good arguments against it.) Hence, the measurement of prejudiced beliefs must be both of their number and their irreversibility. And if we also wish to test for over-generalization, we must know something of the evidence available to the believer, though this is not easy to discover by questionnaire alone. But unless we know this we have no adequate reason for claiming either that the subject is over-generalizing or that he is not.

The upshot of sub-dividing the 'cognitive dimension' in this way is to make highly suspect its status as a single variable. Too many different features are brought under the same heading. The reason why we can say 'too many' is that each of these features of beliefs can, and does, vary independently of the other. The importance, content and over-generalization of a belief do not form a constant cluster of tightly associated properties. Any test or scale which fails to recognize this obvious fact—which treats them jointly as one measurable variable—will not be able to yield us a correct explanation of the variations in scores by respondents. To this criticism it is no defence to say that for each believer there is *some* relationship between the content of his belief, the extent to which he over-generalizes, and the importance he attaches to what he believes. Of course there is, and it may well be an interesting one. But this relationship is different for different people, and different, also, for the distinct beliefs held by the same person. Discovering what this relationship is in one case does not tell us what it is in another. This loose clustering needs further examination. Nevertheless, the complexity and instability of the 'cognitive dimension' is sufficient to prevent it from being the causal partner of the other two dimensions or, indeed, of other 'attitudinal variables'.

The situation is similar when we go on to ask exactly how the emotional and action dimensions are supposed to be related to the cognitive one. These are categories containing emotions, tendencies to action, and beliefs respectively. We know that the relations among these three sorts of factors are complicated, and that if all three are to be measured separately in connection with prejudice the task will be correspondingly difficult. This can be easily illustrated. Suppose, for example, that we wish to measure the amount of fear or envy—instances of the emotional dimension—which the subject has toward a group about whom he holds certain prejudicial beliefs. One, but only one, important way of finding out how fearful he is of that group is to ask him *what* he believes about them: does he believe 'they' are going to attack him in the streets? Does he believe 'they' are trying to replace him in his job? That is, one important test of the strength of his emotion requires that we discover the content of his avowed beliefs. But then testing for the content, and thus the intensity, of his avowed beliefs is here the same procedure as testing for the strength of emotion with which he holds these beliefs. Because the same test will yield both kinds of information, it offers no help in our attempt to devise a *separate* measure of emotional strength, a measure which does not also test for content of avowed belief.

Now to this it may be replied, correctly, that the strength of a particular emotion can be tested in many other ways than by finding out what the agent takes himself to believe. We can investigate, for example, his other emotional states. Thus the strength of the agent's fear of Negroes might be tested by determining how strongly, and frequently, he hoped to avoid them; or by how pleased he was, or by how soothed he became, at the prospect of their absence. We could test his surprise or dismay at meeting Negroes in situations of social intimacy, and we might try to find out how confident he was of being able to control himself in his personal dealings with Negroes. On the other hand, we might investigate the strength of his fear by examining the degree and extent to which it affected his beliefs. One method of doing this would be to find out how ready he was to draw weakly supported conclusions from his fear-based beliefs about Negroes. In those cases in which the agent was prepared to act on such inferences —to act as if those conclusions were true—we should have still another method of testing; for we should be able to look at how he acted, or at how he would have acted, in certain kinds of situations. After all, the reply may continue, many people do not know, in any clear way, *how* strongly they fear (or envy) Negroes. In order to discover this we, and they, have to observe how they behave, what they *do*. A man might believe that his hatred of all Afrikaners was boundless, that it took precedence over all his other dislikes. Nevertheless, he might find that he voted for an Afrikaner in preference to a more liberal candidate because he hated the disappearance of white supremacy even more. It is for cases of this sort that the introduction of the phrase 'action dimension' is useful. It reminds us of the ever-threatening gap between the avowed strength of people's emotions and the strength of those emotions when put to the test of action. True, actions form only one test of strength of emotion, but the test is still important.

However, the fact that we can test for the strength of an emotion in many different ways, including those of belief-content and tendency to action, is not the point at issue. The question is *not* whether prejudiced beliefs, or attitudes, can vary independently in their emotional strength, their propositional content, and their tendency to be expressed in action. No one doubts that they can, or that separate tests for each of these may be devised. The question is whether the three dimensions, *as described*, are three complex properties (natural kinds) whose presence can causally affect each other or affect other properties. The answer for the cognitive dimension has been given already; and the same negative reply holds of the remaining two dimensions. This can be shown quickly.

One property falling under the cognitive 'dimension' was supposed to be that of the importance of the prejudiced belief to the believer; this was one feature included in his 'cognitive orientation'. But the importance of a prejudicial belief to its holder is no different from the tenacity and intensity with which he holds the belief—the degree to which the belief is protected from change or attack, the extent to which it is irreversible. The importance of such a prejudiced belief is the same as the weight given to its retention. For since the belief is defined as argument-resistant, its importance to the believer cannot consist in its weight as a rational consideration. The belief's importance can consist only in its use as a mask for rationality—that is, in the use of the belief so as to express some feeling and emotion. Plainly, the measurement of the importance of the belief under the

48

label 'cognitive dimension' is exactly the same procedure as the measurement of the belief's intensity and persistence under the emotion 'dimension'. So under these two different dimensions we are trying to measure the same features by the same procedure. Thus the importance of the belief—the tenacity and intensity with which it is held—under the label 'cognitive dimension' cannot be a quite different and independent property from the strength of the emotional attitude under the label 'emotional dimension'. Against this conclusion it cannot properly be suggested that measuring the strength of a particular prejudiced belief is quite distinct from measuring the strength of a particular emotional attitude: that since the belief, for example, that all Negroes are physically violent is distinct from the emotion of fear which accompanies that belief, the strength of the former is a separate variable from the strength of the latter. This suggestion misses the point at issue. That point is *not* whether we can distinguish a given belief from its *accompanying* emotion, and hence distinguish their respective strengths. The point is whether in principle we can measure the strength (tenacity and intensity) with which a given prejudicial belief is held without also measuring the strength of the emotional attitude of which that belief is one part, an attitude which the belief expresses. Under the action dimension we can also test for belief importance—by the readiness, type, and variety of actions which also express the emotional attitude in question. But no test of belief-importance can fail to test the emotional attitude of which that belief is a part. Here is sufficient reason for asserting that the three 'dimensions' express a classification which is seriously confused, and so cannot yield a genuine set of three complex properties of prejudice.

3. Dispositions and states as variables

In giving up Kramer's dimensions we also give up their suggested use as variables. And since we have already noticed the lack of clarity in the notion of the authoritarian personality, it is fruitless to go on to investigate the supposed correlations between it and the three 'dimensions'. Whether there be two variables or twenty-one, the entire project is misconceived and doomed from birth. None of these correlations is worth studying unless we are clear about the character of our correlates. Blalock's worries about 'proliferation of dimensions' and 'multi-dimensionality of scales' are amply justified, though not for the reasons he gives, namely, that prejudice and authoritarianism are multi-dimensional (or complexes of properties). There is, instead, a more basic confusion present, a confusion about what constitutes a proper 'dimension', and hence about what constitutes a variable or property suitable for measurement and testing here.

This confusion is brought out by the fact that some of the factors on Blalock's original list—factors such as 'anxiety, frustration, authoritarianism, rigidity, alienation, status concern, conservatism, and conventionalism'—do not lend themselves to treatment as *generic* (rather than specific) personality traits. Yet this is the treatment to which some sociologists have wished to subject them. How, for example, could we possibly define 'conservatism' so as to make the word refer not merely to the agent's political disposition but to a generic personality trait? For a generic trait of personality is a disposition or tendency to exhibit a certain kind, or a tightly knit cluster of kinds, of thought, feeling, and behaviour over an extended period of time and a wide range of activity. But the difficulties of treating 'conservatism' as the name of a *generic* trait are obviously formidable. Many people are conservative in their musical tastes—disliking experimental techniques—and economic radicals. Is it even remotely plausible to suppose that we can go through many of the major fields of human activity so as to classify any given person on some scale of conservatism-radicalism? What could we do with all the scores we would obtain in these various fields? Their simple sum could be of no interest, since a considerable difference in total score between two people might be due to the high conservatism of one person in only a few fields and the moderate conservatism of the other person in all fields. In such a case it would be pointless to claim that the former was more conservative than the latter.

On the other hand, if we tried to obtain the *pattern* of each person's scores, we should only be obtaining a profile of his current attitudes on these topics. This would be of interest only if we had reason to believe that the profile, though not its specific contents, either would not change over time or would change in some regular fashion. For if the profile changed irregularly, or rapidly, or both, it would not be a reliable and accurate indication of the subject's degree of conservatism, of his long-term personality trait. However, our having such a reliable profile would amount to our having a great deal of information that we should not be likely to obtain by questionnaires alone. We should have to know, for example, what crucial items of knowledge and belief were possessed by the subject over long periods of his history. Thus a person might mistakenly come to believe, over a period of time, that many political groups—for instance, the John Birch Society in the United States—were conservative only in appearance, that in fact they were the witting instruments of the Soviet Politbureau and should be banned. As a result, we might find that a person misinformed in this way would alter in his questionnaire score, over an interval of time, from being conservative to being radical. In order to discover that he had not in fact become more radical, we should have to know something about the changes and errors in what he took to be his information: for example, his belief that the John Birch Society was a radical political group.

Even more important with respect to our interest in such score patterns is this. If it were to be a useful trait indicator, we should have to know that the conservative-pattern or profile of the subject was not a mere reflection of, or greatly altered by, his current environment; that it was set and maintained by earlier influences, for example, and that later experiences added little. Otherwise we should be eliciting only his changeable current conservatism, and not his settled conservative trait. But to know that later experiences added little would be to know that the subject, and other people like him in relevant respects, had not changed in generic conservatism despite later rewards, punishments, persuasion, rational argument, or emotional shock. This would fly in the teeth of all experience.

To this it could not properly be replied that what really changes are the person's superficial attitudes and beliefs, but that underlying the subject's conservatism in politics, dress, music, and domestic architecture are certain basic traits which causally determine the less basic and more obvious ones. For if this were so, then these basic traits must make themselves known as conservative or radical by means of their effects, the superficial attitudes which they produce. Yet in agreeing that these effects are altered by all sorts of external current influences—rewards, arguments, punishments—we have already admitted both that our test is merely of superficial, temporary attitudes and that our test itself gives us no grounds for asserting the existence of certain basic traits underlying them. To elicit those basic traits we should need another instrument, and we should need, also, a theory which connected it with the results obtained by the conservatism scale. Either of these alone would not be sufficient. Yet if we had them both, we should clearly have little interest in conservatism in itself as a generic personality trait or in the scale which was supposed to measure it. Instead, we should be interested in the underlying causes of conservatism—the basic traits of which it was an expression —and to these our new instrument would give us access.

But the case of conservatism is only one example of the difficulties which arise from the sociologists' tendency to group together as the names of variables a motley host of terms. The group is motley because the various terms, and often the same term, can be used to refer to quite different kinds of thing. Take, for example, the terms 'anxiety', 'rigidity', and 'frustration'. Each of them can be employed as the name of a dispositional trait or inclination. Some people are prone to develop states in which they are worried, uneasy or apprehensive. Other people are inclined to follow rules to the letter, to dislike exceptions, to avoid situations that require spontaneity; they have, we say, a tendency to be rigid. Still others have a propensity for developing states of thwarted desire in which two of their inclinations are in conflict, or the satisfaction of an inclination is prevented by unfavourable circumstances. Now these three propensities or inclinations to specific states may be interpreted, as we have seen conservatism may be, to apply either to a broader or narrower range of behaviour. We often rely on the context to tell us whether an expression like 'her rigidity' is intended as a reference to a generic character trait or to a more specific inclination, an inclination to be anxious about matters of health, for example. Sometimes, of course, the context—even the sociological context—does not allow us to distinguish. This failure is made more frequent by the sociologist's natural desire to find complex dispositional properties, ones which span a wide variety of activity whose inter-relationships are not obvious at first glance. Knowledge of such complex properties, or natural kinds, is useful, among other reasons, because it gives us inductive grounds for generalizing from the possession of one feature of the kind to the possession of its other features. Depending on how tightly clustered (how unvaryingly associated) the elements of the complex property are thought to be, our argument will take the form: if person A possesses one element of the property in question, it is likely, to some specific degree, that he will also possess the other elements. And once the existence of such a natural kind is established, we are then in a position to try to discover what additional properties in common the members of that natural kind possess. That is, we try to generalize from the fact that one member of the natural kind has a certain additional property to the conclusion that many or most or all members of that natural kind have that property also. We use our knowledge of natural kinds to produce simple laws: to argue, for instance, that if one sample of pure gold dissolves in aqua regia, then all samples of pure gold will do so. The sociologist's desire to find such natural kinds and to employ them in producing law-like generalizations is frustrated, as we now know, by his reliance on policy-dependent terms in their formulation. But the need to find generic dispositional properties is too important to be dropped; and one consequence of this is a tendency by sociologists to turn legitimate specific dispositions into illegitimate generic ones.

However, the terms 'anxiety', 'rigidity' and 'frustration' can be used to refer not to dispositional traits but to states or conditions. A state is a set of items which have specifiable relationships to each other. The duration of a state can be clocked, for it has a beginning and an end. A state also can be generic or specific: thus a wider or smaller variety of different sorts of beliefs, actions, and activities will count toward a person correctly being said to be in one state rather than another. A state of thirst, for example, is more specific than a state of anxiety, because the criteria for the presence of the latter are more varied in type than are those for the presence of the former. Now it is quite easy to fail to distinguish between 'anxiety' or 'rigidity' or 'frustration' when used to refer to *specific* states and those same terms when used to refer to *specific* dispositions.

To say that a person is anxious about his financial future, or that he shows his rigidity by refusing to look at new evidence concerning his wife, or that frustration at work has made him unhappy, is often to leave open the question 'Disposition or state?' A man who is anxious about his financial future may be either in a current state of anxiety or have an inclination to get into such states though not in one at present. A man's refusal to look at new evidence may be interpreted either as a sign of a dispositional trait (rigidity) connected with his marital relations or as a symptom of his current state—his present refusal to change certain views. Similarly, a man may be in an actual state of frustration because of his work or he may merely be showing signs of having a disposition toward such states. We can describe someone as being politically cautious in Australia in 1970, or as being prejudiced against the Japanese now. But these descriptions do not tell us whether the person's state or disposition is being referred to, for he could have been politically cautious or prejudiced in either the dispositional or state sense. He could be in a state of caution or prejudice without having the *tendency* to be either cautious or prejudiced. The more specific the disposition the narrower the range of activity which exemplifies it; and hence the more likely that the disposition and its exemplifying activity will be described and identified by the same set of terms. As Ryle put it:[1]

> the verbs with which we report the different exercises of generic tendencies, capacities and liabilities are apt to differ from the verbs with which we name the dispositions, while the episodic verbs corresponding to the highly specific dispositional verbs are apt to be the same. A baker can be baking now, but a grocer is not described as 'grocing' now, but only as selling sugar now, or weighing tea now, or wrapping up butter now.

This overlap between the terms for specific dispositions and the terms for their exemplifying episodes (or, as we have seen, for their states) produces much confusion. The confusion is made worse when we fail to recognize that there are two distinct types of dispositions, capacities and tendencies, and that the relation of either episodes or states to each of them is somewhat different. Consider, for example, the word 'power', even though it is a generic rather than specific dispositional term.

Max Weber defined 'power' as 'the probability that one actor within a social relationship will be in a position to carry out his own

[1] G. Ryle, *The Concept of Mind*, London, 1949, p. 118.

53

will despite resistance, regardless of the basis on which the probability rests'.[1] This characterization mistakenly identifies the name of a capacity with the likelihood of its being exercised. 'Power', when used dispositionally, is the name of a *capacity* or capability of an agent and is not the name of the likelihood that the agent will be able to exercise that capacity if he wishes. For the phrase 'will be in a position to' simply means 'will have the power to'. So the definition of 'power' will become: 'the probability that one actor within a social relationship will have the power to carry out his own will despite resistance . . .' Here the definiendum reappears within the definiens. Moreover, we cannot interpret 'will have the power to do X' as 'will do X, if he wants to more than anything else and intends to'. This interpretation assumes, in J. L. Austin's words, 'that ability means that opportunity plus motive leads to action.'[2]

Of the many arguments against this assumption we need mention only one. It is that there is an indefinitely large number of intervening conditions which may prevent an ability from being exercised on any given occasion. Their negations will have to be added to wanting and intending as necessary factors for someone doing X, e.g. not being struck dead a moment before. Yet such factors are not part of the *meaning* of the phrase 'power to do X' and so cannot appear in its definition. Thus exercise of power, and hence the likelihood of its exercise, provides evidence that the power is present, but the power may be present without its possessor having any tendency to exercise it. Of course, if he never displays it we shall lack all direct evidence that he has it. Nevertheless, the *sense* (meaning) of a property-name is quite distinct from whatever it is that provides us with our direct *evidence* that the named property exists.

Knowledge that a tendency is present gives us more information than knowledge that only a capacity or capability is present. Tendencies imply capacities, but the latter do not imply the former. Both are expressed in the episodes and states which provide us with evidence of their existence. However, while there can be capacities that remain unexercised even under favourable conditions, there cannot be tendencies which remain unexpressed under such conditions. To possess a tendency is to be prone to act or think or feel in certain ways given certain conditions. If, when those conditions are present, the agent *never* responds in the appropriate manner, there is no tendency of that kind present. We can argue, on theoretical grounds, that the agent would have responded in the required manner if a particular interfering condition had not been present. But in this case we also can describe the conditions under which, if

[1] *The Theory of Social and Economic Organisation*, translated by A. M. Henderson and Talcott Parsons, New York, 1947, p. 152.
[2] 'Ifs and Cans', reprinted in *Philosophical Papers*, Oxford, 1961, p. 175.

they occurred, the tendency *would* be exercised—under which the agent would respond. It does not matter if such favourable conditions seldom occur in fact. What matters is that we be able to show that if they did occur, the tendency would be exercised. This does not hold true of a capacity.

The various distinctions to which we have been referring—those between generic and specific dispositions, between specific dispositions and specific states, between tendencies and capacities—are easily lost sight of when we group together as 'variables' so many different kinds of things. In overlooking some of their important differences we are led to correlate these kinds indiscriminately, and thence to draw unjustifiable inferences about the relationships which either do hold or can hold between our correlated variables. It is not difficult to illustrate some of the problems which are generated by this ambiguity. We need only to turn to some of the studies to which Blalock refers.

4. Srole on characterizing and testing for anomie

One of these studies[1] is an investigation of the hypothesis that the anomie and authoritarianism of individual agents are positively related to the presence of ethnocentrism in those agents. The author's conclusion is that each of the first two variables is significantly and positively related to ethnocentrism (or prejudice against minority groups in particular). Between anomie and authoritarianism there was a Pearson correlation of $+0.45$; between anomie and ethnocentrism a correlation of $+0.43$; and between ethnocentrism and authoritarianism a correlation of $+0.29$. The interesting questions for our purposes, however, lie first, in the descriptions given of these three variables and, second, in the nature of their presumed relationship.

'Anomie' was defined as 'psychic isolation' or 'social mal-integration'. It was tested by means of five statements, each of which was thought to 'represent an important component of the concept'. The first of these components was the agent's view that 'community leaders are detached from and indifferent to his needs'.[2] The test-statement used to represent this view was 'There's little use writing to public officials because often they aren't really interested in the problems of the average man.' The second component was the agent's 'perception of the social order as essentially fickle and unpredictable, i.e. orderless, inducing the sense that under such conditions he can accomplish little towards realizing his future life

[1] L. Srole, 'Social Integration and Certain Corollaries: An Exploratory Study', *American Sociological Review*, 21, 6, 1956, pp. 709–16.
[2] *Ibid.*, p. 712.

goals'.[1] The corresponding statement was 'Nowadays a person has to live pretty much for today and let tomorrow take care of itself.' The third component was the agent's view that 'he and people like him are retrogressing from the goals they have already reached.'[2] The test-statement used was 'In spite of what some people say, the lot of the average man is getting worse, not better.' The fourth component was 'the deflation or loss of internalized social norms or values, reflected in extreme form in the individual's sense of the meaninglessness of life itself'.[3] Representing this was the statement 'It's hardly fair to bring children into the world with the way things look for the future.' The last component was the agent's view that his personal relationships were no longer satisfying. It was expressed by the statement, 'These days a person doesn't really know whom he can count on.'[4]

To each of these statements the respondent was asked to reply either 'I agree', or 'I disagree', or 'I can't decide'. Only the first answer, however, counted toward a score that indicated some degree of anomie.

Our first task here is to scrutinize this account of anomie. The term is being used to refer to 'the breakdown of the individual's sense of attachment to society'.[5] But the use of the term 'breakdown' here is ambiguous. First, it can refer to a *state* which we may characterize by such phrases as 'having broken down', 'having stopped', 'having collapsed'. Second, the term may refer to the event, occurrence or happening which we call *its collapse*. Third, 'breakdown' may be used to refer to the *process of collapsing*. We ought not to confuse a state with an event or with a process, for the three have different properties. Now 'anomie' is obviously not the name of a certain type of event, occurrence, or happening. There are no degrees of an event as there are degrees of anomie, nor can an event consist in the beliefs which are said to be the test-components of anomie. Events are changes in particulars, changes which take place at given times. Thus the belief that the social order is unpredictable cannot be a component of a kind of *event* called 'anomie'. For to believe that something is the case is to be in a certain state or condition, and a state cannot be a component of an event. One state changes to another state, of course, but while this change may be an event which begins a state, the change itself can neither include the state nor be identical with it.

'Anomie' might, however, be taken to be the name either of an entire process or of a state which is part of that process—the process of the individual's increasing estrangement from his society. A

---

[1] *Ibid.*   [2] *Ibid.*, p. 713.
[3] *Ibid.*   [4] *Ibid.*
[5] R. M. MacIver, as quoted in Srole, *op. cit.*, p. 712.

process is a systematic series of connected changes of a property or a set of properties. The series has a datable beginning and end, but it also has a specific result or outcome or end-*state* which terminates the various stages (or states) into which the series is divisible. If anomie is a process, then its measurement consists in determining the extent to which the end-state has been approached or realized by the series of changes that take place in the people who are tested.

The possibilities, then, are these: (a) 'anomie' is a term which refers to the *process* of estrangement undergone by the agent—the alienating of the agent; (b) 'anomie' refers to the end-*state* of that process, the state in which the agent exhibits the property of being totally estranged; (c) the term refers to an earlier state or stage of that process, one in which the agent is partially estranged; (d) the term refers to all three of the preceding items. Now in the paper by Srole he speaks of 'the individual state of anomia' and of 'anomic states'.[1] He also says that 'Each of the five components probably would have been better represented by a series of items comprising a sub-scale.'[2] This latter remark suggests that he may think of each of the components as being itself a sub-process of a total process called 'anomia' so that the remoteness of public officials, for example, could be measured on a sub-scale. Thus it looks as though 'anomia' may be intended to be used as in (d): that is, to refer both to a process and to any state comprised in that process.

But if this interpretation of Srole is correct, then we need to be clear on exactly what is being correlated with authoritarianism and ethnocentrism. The total *process* of anomie cannot by itself be correlated with the two latter traits, for there were no measurements taken of any such process. The scores used were supposed to indicate only that the subjects were more or less anomic, and the total process was otherwise undescribed. So what is being correlated is, in the case of anomie, a range of scores which are thought to measure certain properties of a range of states, or to put it differently, thought to measure certain properties of a number of stages in a vaguely determined process. These are correlated with the episodes (answers) by which the dispositions to ethnocentrism and authoritarianism are supposed to be expressed. States of a condition—stages of a process—are correlated with occurrences of two dispositions. This is taken to show that the more (or less) advanced the agent is in the process, the more (or less) he has those dispositions. The important question, now, is this: how can we tell whether 'anomie' is the name of a 'genuine' condition or process, one which can be causally related to the dispositions of authoritarianism and ethnocentrism—or causally related to occurrences of those

[1] *Op. cit.*, p. 716.   [2] *Ibid.*, p. 713.

dispositions? How can we tell that 'anomie' does not refer only to a pseudo-process?

Clearly, the term 'anomie' will refer to a genuine process only if the fact that a person is in that process allows us to predict, or to retrodict, or to explain, certain features of his behaviour other than his giving particular answers to the test-statements. There must be more to being anomic than simply answering 'I agree' to one or more of those statements. That is, the five statements must be merely a *test* of the presence of the five components and not an exhaustive description of them. For if the latter were the case, we should have an operational *definition* of 'anomie'; and this would result in our being unable to use the term 'anomie' to refer to any piece of behaviour which was not described in the test-statements and, hence, in our being unable to predict or explain anything additional to those descriptions. We must be able to infer from the fact that a person is in a state of anomie under given conditions to a variety of consequences, consequences which do not logically follow from his test-answers.

Thus a great deal depends on the account provided of these expected consequences. The first 'component', for example, was characterized as 'the individual's sense that community leaders are detached from and indifferent to his needs.' Now a person having this belief may tend to display it by doing such things as writing letters of complaint about public officials to newspapers, by refusing to attend political rallies, by refusing to vote, by refusing to pay taxes, or by any of an indefinitely large number of other means. But these other means may also include the exact opposite of the responses just listed: by not writing letters of complaint the agent may be indicating his belief in their ineffectiveness, whereas by attending the leaders' political rallies, and by voting for the opponents of those leaders, he may hope to frustrate them. So this same 'component' (belief) may be displayed by opposite responses. Equally, the same responses may be displays of opposing beliefs, as—in the case of a man who refuses to attend a particular rally for either of two different reasons. The man may refuse to go because he thinks its leaders are indifferent to his desires; or he may refuse to go because he thinks the leaders are responsive enough to feel his absence. How, then, are we to tell, on any given occasion, whether the response is a display of the belief in question?

There are only two ways open to us. The actor can tell us that his response follows from the relevant belief or that it does not. Whether we believe him will depend on what sort of grounds we take ourselves to have for thinking that he is telling the truth. But if he does not tell us, we must rely on additional information about him from which we can infer that he does or does not hold that belief. In the present case, this information will have to be both varied and extensive. For even when we know the specific situation in which he is placed, we must still determine, or assume, that he is rational; that he holds certain beliefs associated with the original belief, for example, that there is nothing he can do to remedy his leaders' indifference; that he has certain desires, goals, and standards of a kind which make the belief in question of some concern to him, since if he is happily unconcerned his response may be quite different.

It is true, of course, that knowing the specific situation in which the agent finds himself will often help us to obtain some of the required information. If a respected school teacher makes a public speech complaining about the apathy of local officials concerning welfare programmes, we may be able to make some reasonable inferences about the relevant desires, goals, beliefs and moral standards which he exhibits. And if these inferences lead us to conclude that he believes the community leaders are indifferent to his needs, and to those of other people similarly placed, we can go on to make certain predictions from the fact that he both has this belief and has particular goals, standards, and accompanying beliefs. We may learn from his speech, or from his speaking out in those circumstances, that he not only believes the community leaders to be indifferent, in general, to community needs, but that he believes that he can help to alter the situation, wishes to do so, and intends to organize a campaign designed to replace the offending leaders. Given this information, we may then predict that he will be a candidate for the local council at the next election.

However, the reasonableness of our prediction here will depend very largely on the reliability and extent of our auxiliary information. For the belief that the agent thinks local leaders indifferent to his needs is so general—can be shown in so many different ways—that its manifestations can be recognized as such only when they are connected to the belief by means of a large body of additional information. In general, the less specific the belief—the more ways in which it can be manifested—the larger the body of auxiliary information which will be needed to correctly identify any given manifestation of that belief. My belief that the Mayor did not read the petition which I presented to him yesterday is quite specific, and since this is only one particular act of one particular leader my belief about it can be shown in far fewer ways than can my belief about all the public acts of all the community leaders. Being displayable in fewer ways, a specific belief can be attributed to an agent by the use of a smaller fund of auxiliary information. For less of it will be required to sort out the smaller number of relationships between response-types and the belief.

This increased difficulty of establishing the presence of a rather general belief by indirect means has obvious consequences for our present example, that of the first component. Here we are trying to use a quite specific statement as a test for the presence of a quite general belief. The connection between the two is so loose that it can only be strengthened by our having a considerable amount of auxiliary information. Yet our procedure of investigation does not give us any way of obtaining it. Replying, 'I agree', to the statement, 'There's little use in writing to public officials because often they aren't really interested in the problems of the average man', is a very weak sign that I take community leaders to be detached from and indifferent to my needs. It becomes a stronger sign to the degree that the respondent interprets the test-statement as asserting the belief in question; to the extent, that is, to which he takes letter-writing to be the most effective means available for communication, public officials to be identical with community leaders, himself to be an average man, and the official's lack of interest to be both irremediable in the long term and of some importance. By our great good luck the respondents may interpret the test-statement in this way, but then all our conclusions will rest, precariously, on this happy chance. Later studies may be less fortunate. Or we can investigate the predictive value of the test response. To do this we shall have to cope, once again, with the problems of auxiliary information. The result will be either that we arrange to increase our information or that we make our belief more specific, or both.

The problem of eliciting the respondent's reasons for his answer to a questionnaire item is neatly illustrated in a case referred to by Richard Christie.[1] A person who happily accepted most of the authoritarian items on the F-scale refused to accept this one: 'War and social troubles may some day be ended by an earthquake or flood that will some day destroy the whole world'. His reason for rejecting this was 'My church says it will be by fire.' Christie comments:[2]

> It seems unlikely that items which have the general vagueness of referents which makes the F scale so uniquely able to capture indigenous authoritarian sentiments could ever be incorporated into an unidimensional scale. Since the items *mean* different things to different people it appears a difficult task to devise items which mean the same things to different individuals for the *same* basic reason.

But since we need to know whether different answers are made for

[1] 'Authoritarianism Re-examined' in *Studies in the Scope and Method of 'The Authoritarian Personality'*, ed. R. Christie and M. Jahoda, Glencoe, Illinois, 1954, p. 139.
[2] *Ibid.*

different reasons, or the same answer for the same reason, there is no substitute for obtaining this information.

There is a further complication which arises for each of the five components of anomie. They are all described as being *beliefs* of the agent: as his 'perception' of some state, of his 'sense that' something is the case, or his 'view that' such-and-such is true. Clearly, none of these beliefs, in so far as they refer to social conditions, need be correct. But if 'anomie' is defined as the holding of these beliefs, their correctness or falsity with respect to actual conditions should be immaterial to the presence of the agent's alienation. However, these components have been selected by Srole to 'represent internalized counterparts or reflections, in the individual's life situation, of conditions of social dysfunction'.[1] If any part of the beliefs about social conditions is false, we shall have to decide whether the respondent is, to that extent, in a condition of anomie even though there is no corresponding condition of social dysfunction. To answer that he is not then in a state of anomie will be to preserve the supposed link between individual anomie and social dysfunction. The cost of doing this will be the admission that the link is mere conjecture; no part of the investigation is directed toward establishing such a connection. All that the investigation can show, at best, is that the respondents hold certain beliefs. Whether or not any of these is true cannot be discovered from the fact that all of them are held.

On the other hand, if we sever the connection and agree that the investigation tests only for beliefs, then we jettison the topic with which the author began. For of 'central interest', he says, 'are the individuals entering adulthood as "normal" personalities but in whom anomia develops in response to objective conditions of stressful malintegration in their social worlds'.[2] Since testing for an agent's *beliefs* about his social integration is different from testing for his social integration, a presumed link between the two might be suggested on the ground that the presence of the agent's beliefs is good evidence of their truth. But this will have to be shown by a further, and independent, study. Nor does it help to reply that a person is socially unintegrated to the extent that he thinks of himself as being so. For unless his belief 'develops in response to objective conditions of stressful malintegration' in his society, it shows us nothing about his society's condition, and hence nothing about his actual relationship to it. To take a person's belief in his lack of social integration as logically entailing that he is not socially integrated is simply to reiterate, by means of a definition, that anomie does not have to correspond with social dysfunction. And in claiming this, we again sever the link between them rather than strengthen it, as the reply set out to do.

[1] *Op. cit.*, p. 712.   [2] *Ibid.*, p. 711 n. 9.

Yet once we grant that 'anomie' is to be defined as the holding of one or more of the five component-beliefs, a number of consequences follows which alters the interpretation of Srole's argument. 'Anomie' can no longer be the name of a social process by which the agent is increasingly estranged from his society. The term 'anomie' will have to name a rather different process, a purely psychological one in which the agent holds, to an increasing extent, *beliefs* about his estrangement from other people. The importance of this change is that it puts into question the original choice of the five components of anomie. We know that they were supposed to be those which 'on theoretical grounds would represent internalized counterparts or reflections, in the individual's life situation, of conditions of social dysfunction'. If they are no longer to be counterparts of social dysfunction, on what theoretical grounds is the choice of them to rest?

The five components may well be the components of psychological isolation, and anyone in this state will be weakly attached to society, will fail to identify with other people, will feel 'alone, cut off, unwanted, unloved, unvalued'.[1] But the investigator's choice of the five components cannot be determined merely by his view that they make up a state of psychological isolation. For such a state can be the causal outcome of a great number of pathological conditions, and it would be pointless here to test for the presence of that state unless the investigator also put forward some view as to its cause. Psychological isolation is such a common effect or symptom that, taken by itself, its positive correlation with authoritarianism and ethnocentrism will tell us nothing specific. We might as well try to correlate the presence of blood-shot eyes in men with their joint alcohol consumption and hours of sleep. Some blood-shot eyes are produced by drinking and sleeplessness and some are not. Similarly, it may be plausible to suggest that some kinds of psychological isolation—namely, those which express social anomie—are causally related to authoritarianism and ethnocentrism. It is not plausible to suggest that all kinds of psychological isolation are so related, for we already know that they are not. Knowing this, our choice of the five components must be guided by some view as to their source, a source through which they can be related to such factors as authoritarianism. Without some view as this, we have no grounds either for choosing these particular components or for investigating these particular correlations.

Now to all this it must be added that our criticism has not mentioned an important distinction which, according to Robert Merton,[2]

---

[1] Srole, *op. cit.*, p. 712, quoting Harold Lasswell, 'The Threat to Privacy', in R. M. MacIver (ed.), *Conflict of Loyalties*, New York, 1952.

[2] 'Anomie, Anomia and Social Interaction: Contexts of Deviant Behavior', in *Anomie and Deviant Behavior*, M. B. Clinard (ed.), New York, 1964, p. 227.

was proposed first by Srole: the distinction between the normlessness of a social system—the failure of certain social standards to be accepted as legitimate—and the psychological state of the people living in that society, their feeling that there are no accepted social standards. The former is to be called 'anomie', the latter 'anomia'. Srole's questionnaire, then, was supposed to measure anomia and not anomie, although the two are connected in various ways. In fact, Merton has suggested that once we determined what proportion of the population had a particular degree of anomia we should then have an index of anomie for that social unit.[1]

But it is clear that the distinction between anomie and anomia— between a normless society and anomic feelings—is the very one which is straddled in Srole's account. Individual anomia, as tested by his scale, was assumed to develop as a response to social anomie. Yet this assumption is nowhere established by Srole, or anyone else; in fact, it is highly unlikely to be true.[2] Introducing the term 'anomia' only makes the need for a causal connection between anomia and anomie—the individual state and the social condition—more obvious. It also makes the significance of the supposed correlation between anomia and ethnocentrism even more obscure, since so much turns on whether anomia is produced by anomie.

The conclusion of our present argument is this: because 'anomie' is defined solely in terms of the agent's beliefs, we both lose the link with social dysfunctions and make it impossible, given our procedure of investigation, to use the ascription of anomie as a means of predicting the agent's behaviour. Once we are deprived of our ability to predict or retrodict anomic behaviour, we also lose our ability to test the cash value, or empirical content, of the notion of anomie; and having lost that, we have no way of showing that the term 'anomie' refers to either a genuine process or state. Under these conditions it is useless to determine the correlations between the response to the anomie test and any other test. It is especially point-less to correlate responses of the former kind with those of the F-scale for authoritarianism, since the F-scale, as we have seen, embodies many unsolved difficulties of its own. Correlation of the responses to these two tests merely buries the diverse problems of each test in a common grave from which disinterment becomes still more difficult.

---

[1] *Ibid.*, p. 229.
[2] See the pointed criticisms in 'Psychological Dimensions of Anomy', H. McClosky and J. H. Scitaar, *American Sociological Review*, 30, February 1965, pp. 14–40.

Chapter four

1. Inadequate criteria of application

We have been discussing a number of the problems connected with the definition of some typical terms of sociology: 'prejudice', 'authoritarian personality', 'conservatism', 'anomie'. In consequence, we have also been discussing both the character of the complex properties to which these terms are supposed to refer, and the adequacy of certain procedures used for locating and measuring these supposed properties. It is now time to answer the question with which our discussion began. That question was, 'What useful suggestions for obtaining definitions of theoretical significance can we extract from a sample of the present practice of sociologists?' In short, what aid can we obtain from the examples that we have been considering?

One point is clear immediately. All the examples with which we have been concerned—the studies of prejudice, authoritarianism, and anomie—fail our earlier requirement for useful scientific criteria. For in these studies no serviceable tests of prejudice, authoritarianism, and anomie are provided. The properties in question are not identifiable by scientifically acceptable means nor are they shown to be associated with reliable indicators. In the case of prejudice the difficulty arose, in part, from its mischaracterization as merely an 'unsubstantiated, firmly held prejudgment of individuals and groups'. This phrase omits any reference to the vital feature of unreasonable retention of judgment. Another problem arose from the claim that there are 'cognitive, emotional and evaluative dimensions of prejudice' which can be measured independently of each other. Since this claim is false, no adequate test of prejudice is derivable from it. The case of authoritarianism is similarly difficult. The supposed test (the F-scale) is such an unsatisfactory measure of authoritarianism that we are left with no acceptable way of identifying the presence

64

of that supposed property. Moreover, the defects of the F-scale indicate corresponding defects in the original characterization of the authoritarian personality, since the factor analysis of 'the three basic properties' in that personality shows them to be dispensable. Thus the analysis also shows that the description originally given of authoritarianism has little useful application.

Much the same can be said of Srole's treatment of anomie. The A-test statements are not only poor measures of the five components of anomie, but the use of the test indicates that the characterization of the five components themselves does not give us a scientifically useful description of a social process. For either the components are merely beliefs of the agent or they are the unsubstantiated counterparts, in the agent, of social dysfunctions. In either case we are provided with no acceptable means of identifying and measuring social dysfunction as it is expressed in certain beliefs of individual agents.

If social malintegration is that psychic isolation of the individual which is caused by social dysfunctions, then both the isolation and the dysfunctions must be recognizable by means of the procedures available to us. And the supposed causal connection between them must be supported by evidence. Thus we shall need tests for the presence of such dysfunctional features as: the detachment of community leaders; the unpredictability of the operation of institutions; the loss of status, income, and power; and whichever other social conditions are taken to be both operative and dysfunctional. We shall also need corresponding measures of the isolating effects of these conditions on the respondents. Two possible effects are those mentioned earlier, namely, the rejection of social norms by the agent, and his belief that personal relationships are no longer satisfying to him. In addition, we must be able to identify any other acts or beliefs which are defining characteristics of his emotional isolation. These characteristics may or may not include the person's *beliefs* that community leaders are detached, that institutional operations are unpredictable, that he has lost income, status, and power. If the presence of these or other beliefs, or of certain acts, is taken as a test of the respondent's isolation, we must then be able to produce evidence that their presence is the causal result of the relevant dysfunctional conditions.

With a notion as complex as that of anomie, to list all these requirements is to despair of meeting them *in practice*. Any condition which is describable as 'fickleness and unpredictability in the social order' does not offer us much in the way of distinctive features for its recognition. And since so many different kinds of events and situations might count as instances of it, the supposed condition will have to be redescribed before we can use its occurrence as a distinguishing mark of anything else. The same sort of vagueness and generality will have to be eliminated from the descriptions of the other marks of anomie. Yet the difficulties are so formidable that we must ask why the effort to overcome them is thought to be worth while and how we could decide whether it is in fact justifiable.

Srole thought of individual anomie (or anomia) as an intervening variable between an independent variable (social dysfunction) and a dependent variable (behaviour change).[1] The presence of anomie was supposed to explain how certain social dysfunctions produced certain personality changes. A deterioration in the social bonds was thought to create 'self-to-others alienation' in the members of the group, and this psychic isolation of each member was supposed to explain his subsequent change of behaviour. The point of correlating the presence of anomie with that of ethnocentrism and authoritarianism was that the latter two traits were taken to be 'escape reactions' to the individual's anomie. Thus underlying the investigation was an implicit hypothesis to the effect that people in general dislike being in a state of anomie; ethnocentrism and authoritarianism are two of their characteristic ways of trying to overcome anomie; and that these ways are characteristic because they seem to offer hope of strengthening some of the social bonds which have been weakened in the anomic state.

Now it is obvious that if 'anomie' is not given adequate criteria of application, neither this hypothesis nor the correlation with ethnocentrism and authoritarianism can come to anything. For both depend, in an essential way, on our being able to meet at least these requirements: (1) an acceptable procedure for independently identifying the presence of each trait; (2) a procedure for identifying their joint presence; (3) evidence that the syndrome actually occurs in some population, and in the case of a genetic property like that of 'authoritarianism', (4) evidence of a causal connection between childhood treatment and the adult syndrome. Again, if we had no evidence of a causal connection between social dysfunctions and psychic isolation, and thus no sound reason to assume such a relation, authoritarianism could not play the part assigned to it in the hypothesis. Since there would be no link between social malfunctioning and individual anomie, there could be no attempted restorative such as authoritarianism. And without this hypothesis, or some substitute for it, we should have no good reason for testing the correlation between anomie and authoritarianism.

Hence, the attempt to give adequate criteria of application for 'anomie' is worth while to the extent that it is required in the formulation and testing of a worth-while hypothesis. But to say this is merely

[1] *Op. cit.*, p. 716.

66

to repeat in different words what was said at the end of the previous chapter: that a useful operational specification is one which refers to measurable properties of theoretical interest. The question whether it is in fact justifiable to try to recast Srole's definition of 'anomie' comes down to the question whether the success or failure of Srole's hypothesis—or some substitute for it—will make a significant contribution to our knowledge. Does anything which substantially affects the rest of sociology hang on the truth or falsity of that hypothesis? If we answer 'yes' we thereby have given a justification for trying to respecify 'anomie'.

The truth, however, is that neither anomia nor anomie will bear the sociological weight which has been placed on them. Both are sets of conditions which result from many different sorts of causes, psychological and social. To treat either anomia or anomie as a specific condition arising from specific causes is to manufacture a pseudo-concept. Each of them classifies together a large number of different kinds of events which have nothing in common but the property of causally resulting from various social malfunctions. In this respect their role is similar to that of the term 'juvenile delinquency'. The latter, wrote J. A. Mack, 'is a convenient classificatory device bringing together a great variety of pieces of behaviour which have no characteristic in common other than that they will, if detected and dealt with by the police, bring the subject of the behaviour into Court on a criminal charge.'[1] Or as E. M. Lemert put it: 'Whether given behaviour of a youth is described as delinquent . . . depends upon the perception of arresting officers, availability of biographical data, estimates of the morality of his parents, monetary claims of victims, the biases in judges, and therapeutic ideologues of probation officers and social workers.'[2]

2. Adequate criteria and problem formulation

It is commonly, and correctly, said that many sociologists oscillate between measuring insignificant properties and constructing grandiose but untestable theories. It is less commonly asked why this oscillation occurs. To this question the example of anomie can help to contribute an answer. We have only to recall that Srole's definition of 'anomie' was both very sketchy and very ambitious. It assumed the truth of an important generalization—that social dysfunctions cause psychological isolation—without providing any acceptable means of formulating, and hence testing, it. The questionnaire used to test for anomie did not in fact do so; if it tested for anything, it

[1] 'Juvenile Delinquency Research: A Criticism', *Sociological Review*, 3, 1955, p. 57.
[2] 'Social Structure, Social Control, and Deviation' in Clinard, *op. cit.*, p. 95.

tested for the presence of certain beliefs whose connection with each other was not established and whose significance was dubious. In brief, the definition of 'anomie' itself encapsulated the oscillation between insignificance and untestability with which sociologists are charged. Any hypothesis that employed this definition could not help but produce an explanation in which these defects were embedded. The measurement of insignificant properties is simply the complement of the construction of untestable theories, for each produces the other. Many theories are untestable because their property-terms are not adequately defined or are not given adequate criteria of application; and many properties are insignificant because the terms which refer to them are not part of the vocabulary of a testable theory.

How, then, can this oscillation be stopped? The full answer to this question must wait upon later discussion, since the answer we give depends on what we think is wrong with the generalizations and explanatory accounts offered by recent sociologists. However, it is worth enlarging now on one point made at the end of the previous chapter. It can be summarized in this way: the adequacy of the criteria of application (or operational specification) of a property-term is crucially dependent on the successful formulation of the problem in whose solution that term is employed. This is a very modest claim because operational specifications are proposed for specific tasks, and those tasks are set by the formulation of problems. But since not all such problems require the use of the technical definitions—for we may use the terms of daily life—there is *some* purpose in making the claim. Criteria of application are dependent on problem-characterization even in those cases where the converse is not true.

Now one, but only one, necessary condition of phrasing a problem well is the compatibility, both logical and empirical, of its assumptions. This condition is not met by Srole's study. For if we take 'authoritarianism' as the causal result of 'a history of strict treatment in childhood', how can this kind of authoritarianism also be an 'escape reaction' to anomie—an attempt by the agent to restore weakened social bonds? It has never been suggested by anyone that parents, either deliberately or inadvertently, reared their children as authoritarians in order that they or their children might restore those bonds. On the other hand, if authoritarianism is not genetically defined, it is still subject to all the earlier criticism, with this addition: 'authoritarianism' becomes the name of a set of traits which is sometimes, but not always, produced by anomie, and sometimes produced by other, unknown conditions. In short, authoritarianism, like boredom, can be caused by many different sorts of situation. Explaining, in general, why some people become authoritarian will be no more useful, and no more specific, a solution than explaining why some people become bored.

Since criteria of application so closely reflect problem-characterizations, it is no surprise that Srole's treatment of 'anomie' is unsatisfactory. To recapitulate: the notion was intended to express the agent's sense of his lack of integration with the social system. Yet no clear procedure is suggested for distinguishing a case of a non-integrated person from an integrated one. Nor are we told whether a person might think that he was integrated (or not), but be mistaken. It is important to know whether the agent is supposed to be the only judge in the matter, or only the final judge, or neither. Our criteria of integration will be very different according to which of these three alternatives is chosen.

The reason why this difficulty is present here is that the terms 'integration' and 'malintegration' themselves were not introduced into the literature to help solve a specific empirical problem. They were introduced as suggestive dummy-terms in the course of theoretical discussions about social systems. Thus the term 'integration' has been used to refer, on the one hand, to social solidarity or allegiance, and on the other hand, to the way in which a set of social activities is so organized that each one can be carried out properly.[1] In the first sense, 'malintegration' refers to the agent's lack of support for, or loyalty to, the social organization of his group. In the second sense, 'malintegration' refers to the defective ordering of social activities and to impediments which prevent them from being carried out properly. The former comes close to being 'self-to-others alienation'; the latter being social dysfunction.

This ambiguity is not only responsible for muddling together two different empirical problems—the measurement of alienation and the measurement of defective ordering—it may also be responsible for Srole's unsatisfactory definition of 'anomie'. For in identifying it with socially produced alienation (psychic isolation caused by social dysfunction), Srole may have run together the two senses of 'malintegration' under the heading 'anomie', or 'anomia'. The connection between them may have remained obscure because their partnership was the result of this confusion. And this confusion would then have infected both the underlying hypothesis and the study of the correlations with ethnocentrism and authoritarianism. Thus 'anomie' would have been badly defined because its characterization incorporated an unrecognized problem rather than having been drawn up with a view to solving a recognized one.

The importance of stating the problem is made clear if we recall the way in which Srole described the claim he wished to test: 'social

[1] A distinction made by H. Fallding in *The Sociological Task*, Englewood Cliffs, New Jersey, 1968, p. 114.

69

malintegration, or anomia, in individuals is associated with a rejective orientation toward out-groups in general and toward minority groups in particular.'[1] Obviously, the testing of this claim is of much less interest if we are merely testing for correlation than if we are trying to obtain evidence about some underlying hypothesis which will account for the association between anomia and ethnocentrism or for some feature of other, related properties. In that case, however, the claim should be presented as a logical consequence of that hypothesis, a consequence whose truth or falsity will either help to confirm or disconfirm the hypothesis. Srole's failure to make this explicit—and the failure of many other sociologists to do this—disguises the character of the investigation. It makes the testing of an inexplicit hypothesis look like an attempt simply to find a causal connection between certain changes in properties by first determining the correlations between the measure of those properties. But if the character of the investigation were made plain, the deficiencies of the hypothesis would be equally plain and the entire project would be reconsidered.

The previous chapter ended with a question which we have been pursuing here under various guises. The question was 'How ought we to go about the production of operational specifications that have a theoretical point?' We can now give a short and clearly unhelpful answer: 'By producing testable answers to properly phrased questions'. The ways in which questions can fail to be properly phrased are many, but if we think of our earlier examples we can remind ourselves of at least one more of the characteristic defects. The simplest and most obvious variety of it consists merely in forgetting, for the moment, that determining an appropriate answer to a question always depends on determining to which problem the question is relevant. Neglect of this leads to imaginary dilemmas like the one in which Blalock found himself when he wrote: 'One of the problems in measuring discrimination is that of identifying the unit to be measured. Is it the number of discriminatory *acts*, the number of discriminatory actors, or the number of persons affected by discrimination?'[2] Whether we wish to measure the number of acts, actors, or patients will depend on which measurement helps to solve our problem. Thus, if our problem is to find out what proportion of the unemployed labour force is due to discriminatory hiring, we shall measure the number of persons affected and not the number of discriminatory employers.

A somewhat more interesting failure of the same kind is exhibited when we ask the question 'What personality features help causally to determine the presence of the prejudiced opinions held by groups of people?' Suppose we take prejudiced opinions to consist, as we

[1] *Op. cit.*, p. 712.   [2] *Op. cit.*, p. 17n.

did earlier, in adverse beliefs, impervious to correction by rational argument alone, concerning the members of other social groups. What, then, do we wish to know in asking whether such personality features as anxiety, authoritarianism, status concern, conventionalism, or rigidity are causal contributors to the existence and maintenance of such adverse beliefs?

We cannot, on the one hand, be asking why *any* person *anywhere* ever holds such adverse beliefs and, on the other hand, give as our suggested answer one or more of the personality features just listed. For it seems obvious that in many societies these beliefs are simply passed on to each generation of children by their elders. In such societies the more fruitful question to ask may be 'Why do a few people here *not* hold these prejudiced opinions? Why has the learning process not been completely successful?' So at the very least we must have in mind a situation in which certain adverse beliefs of a particular kind are held by some groups and not by others. Our problem will be that of accounting for the difference either in the kind or in its members. Our answer will be that people of the prejudiced group are *more* anxious or *more* conventional or *more* rigid than people of the unprejudiced group. We shall have to assume, of course, that the two groups have had much the same opportunities to learn these particular prejudices; and we shall have to assume, also, that we have available a hypothesis which explains how increased anxiety or conventionality or rigidity are causally connected with prejudiced beliefs. But this is hardly enough. Imagine that it is only certain prejudices of a particular type whose appearance we can try to explain. Then we must account for the presence here of these particular prejudices alone rather than some of the alternatives. How is this to be done?

One way, obviously, is for us to know that there are no alternatives, that the two groups share all prejudices except one of the relevant type. This happy situation is unlikely to occur if psychological theories of prejudice formation are correct. For the same mechanism which produces a dislike of one out-group will also produce a dislike of other out-groups. Very few societies cannot muster more than one such target. And since it is a psychological hypothesis which we are now considering, the correctness of the hypothesis will ensure that the two groups differ in more than one prejudice toward out-groups. Hence we must still explain why the two groups differ in just these prejudices of the same type.

Another way of accounting for these particular differences is to argue that, in addition to the psychological property, another factor is needed to produce the contrast between the two groups, although that factor is not yet known. Our psychological property will be a cause of prejudiced opinions in the sense that it is a necessary part

F

of one complex sufficient but unnecessary condition. In the absence of the psychological property, the remainder of the conditions would not have produced the prejudice, even though some other sufficient condition might then have done so. The unknown factor will be a similarly indispensable part of the same sufficient but unnecessary condition. But to argue in this fashion we must be clear about the causal field in which prejudices sometimes appear and sometimes do not. We must know, for example, whether our question is 'What *now* produces specific prejudiced beliefs of a certain kind in people belonging to this industrial society, since earlier these people lacked such beliefs?' The causal field here is the history of this society within which prejudiced beliefs were first absent and then present— a difference we wish to explain. Or is our question 'What produces these beliefs in people belonging to this particular contemporary industrial society when the beliefs are absent in people of other contemporary industrial societies?' Here the causal field is that of contemporary industrial societies, and we wish to know what difference among such societies accounts for the existence of these beliefs. Each of these questions may be generalized to refer to *kinds* of industrial society. The first question will become one about change of belief in a certain kind of society; the second question will be about change of belief between people of one kind of industrial society and those of another kind.

The importance of knowing which causal field our question assumes is this: if we are to have a practical method of discovering causal connections we must assume that the cause can be located among a limited group of conditions thought to be relevant. Without our relying on this assumption, we should not know where to begin looking for the cause. But in order to obtain such a limited group— even by merely looking in the temporal and spatial vicinity of the effect—we must know the causal field. We must know, for example, whether to look for possible causes in the history of a particular society or in the current conditions of contemporary societies of a certain kind. Obviously, our being clear about which causal field is in question will be necessary though not sufficient to enable us to form a satisfactory group of conditions, conditions which may be relevant. The difficulty, then, in arguing that in addition to a psychological property another unknown factor will be required, is that the nature of the causal field is the very point at issue. If our original question about the causal role of personality features in the existence of prejudices had indicated the causal field, we should not have been able to use that question as a cautionary example. Failure to indicate the causal field is an elementary way of not phrasing a problem adequately. For that reason its prevalence in sociological studies is both important and deplorable.

3. The mis-use of variable analysis

Our examples have been chosen to show that there is a deadly and reciprocal set of relations which hold among pseudo-properties, untestable theories, and ill-phrased problems. One of these examples had its origin in the question whether any person who displays 'unsubstantiated, firmly held, prejudgments of individuals and groups' also displays certain other personality features which cause him to hold those prejudices. This question, we have been arguing, is ill formed, unfruitful in its outcome, and yet characteristic of many others in the field of sociology. The reason why it is characteristic is simple. It belongs to a class of questions which arise from the *misuse* of a particular method of sociological investigation; that method consists in the establishment and analysis of correlations among variables whose distribution is determined by surveys and questionnaires.

The temptation to mis-use originates in the fact that there are almost no limitations on what can be correlated with what. Variables can be formed from such diverse sources as: death rates, 1916–19, of adult men in Chicago; length of high school education, current rate of unemployment among Swedish accountants; the changing volume of British migration to Australia; the incidence of hospitalized psychotics. The list is endless. Because it is, the use of surveys and the statistical analysis of their variables, as a means of locating significantly high positive or negative correlations, is common. But since there are statistical procedures for eliminating high spurious correlations—those which, on the evidence assumed, cannot be signs of causal connection—it is also common to try to locate causally significant correlations in the absence of any directly relevant theoretical background. Having discovered such an apparently causal correlation the sociologist must then go on to produce an explanatory hypothesis which can be tested. The difficulty, and hence the danger, is twofold.

First, when correlation hunting precedes hypothesis formation in this way, the specifications (criteria of application) are not suggested by the hypothesis which is to account for the correlation. The criteria are suggested by common sense and common belief, by the terminology of the technical material from which the variables were drawn, or by covert hypotheses. All these are unsatisfactory, since both what we want to explain and how we describe it are largely determined by the hypothesis which guides us, wittingly or unwittingly. If we rely on common sense, or a covert hypothesis, our explicandum and its description will be set for us by beliefs which we have not examined. That is, our problem will be produced from a background of hypotheses of which we are aware only in part and whose truth remains untested. But then we have correspondingly little assurance that the problem is likely to be a worthwhile or fruitful one. It may arise, for example, from false presuppositions and the hypothesis used to supply an answer may be wasted. The trouble with mere correlation hunting is that it often puts us in this position. Since we are investigating without benefit of a clear and testable hypothesis, we have too few constraints on the descriptions or specifications of our variables. Because there is no way of determining the adequacy of these descriptions in terms of a purpose at hand, there is no way of improving them or of finding out what is wrong with them other than by supplying such a purpose in the form of one or more explanatory hypotheses. However, these will arrive too late on the scene to help in formulating the problem or characterizing the explicandum. So either the problem (the correlation) will be accepted at face value, or criticism of it will have to begin with the sources and theoretical background from which the problem arose. The first alternative may well be misleading or mistaken; the second alternative does not benefit from the advantage which correlation discovery was supposed to confer—that of producing a worth-while explicandum.

Second, the number of statistically significant (high) correlations, like the number of possible variables, is indefinitely large. And since a great many variables concern specific times and places, a very large number of those correlations which later turn out to be causally significant will be expressible not as *universal* causal statements, but as *general* causal statements. They will assert that a given limited set of situations of a certain sort at a particular time and place was caused by another limited set of situations of a specific sort, time, and place. These *general* statements will take the form 'The abnormally high death rates of adult men in Chicago, 1917–19, were caused by the war-time shortage of medical staff and facilities.' But the accumulation of general causal statements is of no great interest to a scientist unless those statements bear on some hypothesis or theory: that is, unless they are derivable from it, are tests of it, or pose a problem for it. Otherwise, they simply join the vast collection of general causal statements which we believe to be true, statements like 'The lungs of all the residents of Bramble Street are being damaged by fumes from the local oil refinery.' So the mere fact that a statement of correlation is shown later to be expressible as a general causal statement need not be of any *scientific* significance. We need some reason for thinking that any given correlation, whether high or low, is of scientific interest to us. And this reason is usually provided, either directly or indirectly, by an hypothesis or a theory. Since correlation-hunting 'on spec' gives us no such reason, it has to be supplied later as best we can.

Sometimes we use an hypothesis to explain the presence of a known correlation and sometimes to predict the occurrence of a previously unknown one. This does not matter. Both procedures use the hypothesis to pick out the significant correlation. Nor does it matter, in this respect, that the descriptions of the variables often embody complex hypotheses themselves, as in the case of anomie or that of television influence on juvenile delinquency. The fact that in such cases we are looking neither for *general* causal statements nor for *universal* ones (in the shape of simple law-like regularities) is important. For when we look for correlations *between* law-like regularities it becomes less plausible to think of these correlations as signs of direct causal connections. We are forced to consider the possibility of an indirect connection like that between the movements of the tides, the acceleration of falling bodies, and the revolution of the earth around the sun. This connection can be provided only by a theory.

It is, of course, no criticism of the method of variable analysis that some sociologists have failed to observe its limitations. Nor can its mis-use be made responsible for all the different ways in which sociological problems can fall short of adequate formulation. Nevertheless, the impulse to try to discover social laws by means of correlation-hunting remains strong among sociologists. It is an impulse which remains strong because confirmed empirical hypotheses and laws are in short supply, and variable analysis based upon survey data seems to offer an *independent* method of determining where likely prospects may be found. Since, however, there is no such independent method, sociologists who wish, like other *scientists*, to produce criteria of application for terms that refer to genuine properties have no option. They must produce testable universal and statistical hypotheses, and if possible go on to produce the statements of empirical laws which these hypotheses are intended to foreshadow.

To this assertion the reply has often been made that sociologists have tried for a long time to do just that and have not succeeded. There must be, then, a deeper reason for their apparent failure than the ones which we have touched on. It must be, so the reply goes, that sociology is not, and cannot become, a generalizing *science* after all. The search for universal social laws is hopelessly misguided, and this explains all the deficiencies in sociology which we have been considering: pointless definitions, pseudo-properties, and now, the absence of empirical laws.

To answer this charge directly would be to step on a treadmill best left to those who enjoy the exercise because they have nowhere else to go. The charge derives its plausibility from the twin assumptions that sociology as practised is irremediably defective, and that the existence of these defects is most adequately explained by their irremediable source. Most sociologists do not take either assumption seriously, for they believe, quite correctly, that successful counter-examples are ready to hand. But it does not follow that some other explanation of the apparent scarcity of testable hypotheses and empirical laws is without value. Why, indeed, should there be even an appearance of short supply? To that question we must now turn.

Generalizations

Chapter five

1. The utility of Blalock's two principles

Of all the charges levelled at sociologists, perhaps the most common and most harsh is that their generalizations are either tautologically true or plainly false. It is common because many sociologists themselves are not clear as to what a well-formed universal hypothesis would look like; but it is harsh because no aid is given. The source of the difficulty is either said to be so deep-seated that sociological generalization is impossible, or attributed to such superficial causes— like the complexity of the relations among the numerous variables —that their supposed effect is mystifying. Since the two diagnoses are equally unhelpful, the corresponding prognoses are equally doctrinaire. For the one party, a generalizing sociology has no future. For the other party, sociologists stand permanently on the brink of success. Neither party can help us here.

What will be of use, however, is for us to consider, in detail, some examples of the generalizations about which we complain. The usefulness of doing this will not lie in our producing new instances of an excessively familiar fault. It will lie in our attempt to find in the details of these examples an answer to the question, 'Why is this fault so common? What circumstances impel sociologists, again and again, to bring forward as empirical hypotheses a set of candidates which are either trivially true or obviously false?' If we can answer this question, we may be in a better position to explain why plausible general hypotheses seem to be in short supply. It may turn out, for example, that the conditions which account for the abundance of unsatisfactory candidates also account for the apparent shortage of satisfactory ones.

For our source of examples we can retain Blalock's book, *Toward a Theory of Minority-Group Relations*. Many other studies would serve equally well, but this one has the great advantage of explicitly stating and sensibly discussing a large number of related theoretical propositions. As Blalock rightly says, 'This must be done even though the empirical evidence may be only suggestive and based on very restricted or atypical populations. At this stage, the exact wording of the propositions does not seem crucial, though once we begin to work with a delimited number of variables more careful attention must be given to this question.'[1] Later on he adds that 'the qualifying phrase "other things being equal" should be understood' to apply in all cases.[2] Blalock also says that his propositions are intended to be 'statistical regularities of the form, "the greater the X, the greater the Y".' This means that Y is dependent on X and not vice versa.[3]

Before advancing his first set of theoretical propositions, Blalock makes an introductory remark of some interest, for it contains in miniature the problem with which we are concerned. He is discussing how a goal-seeking agent will select the means he takes to be most efficient:[4]

> I would expect that the more important the goal relative to others, the greater the tendency to prefer means that maximize the probability of success as compared with means that minimize the expenditure of resources. To the degree that progress toward the goal is difficult to assess, and therefore efficiency also hard to determine, I would predict a tendency to prefer means that minimize the expenditure of resources ('the easy way out').

Now it is obvious that the first sentence quoted is in serious danger of being interpreted as trivially true. The phrase 'the more important the goal relative to others' may well be taken to *mean* 'the more we prefer to achieve the goal relative to others'. Then in expecting a consequential increase in the *tendency to prefer* maximizing means, Blalock is on peculiarly safe ground. For it would be self-contradictory to say that an increasingly greater *tendency to prefer* success-maximizing means, rather than resource-conserving means, to goal A, did not accompany the increasing importance of—increasing preference for—goal A relative to other goals. If there were not an increasingly greater *tendency to prefer* such means, what could the phrase 'increasing preference for A' possibly mean? It is not claimed that the means are actually used, but that they are *preferred* increasingly. Can a goal become more important to us while we have no greater *tendency to prefer* the means likely to achieve it? If so, then the greater importance of the goal will not lead us to tend to pursue it increasingly, will not motivate us more in this respect than do other goals. Yet the whole point of the discussion from which the quoted sentence comes is that sociologists must estimate the differing

---

[1] *Op. cit.*, p. 35.   [2] *Ibid.*, p. 48.
[3] *Ibid.*   [4] *Ibid.*, p. 39.

degrees to which different kinds of goals motivate us—lead us to pursue them. By defining 'goal importance' independently of the tendency to prefer success-maximizing means, we should be abandoning our interest in degree of motivation.

The assertion made in the second sentence of the quotation is not clear. Is progress toward the goal difficult to assess because the goal is vague or because the productivity of the means is difficult to determine? If the latter, then why should there be a tendency to prefer minimum expenditure? If the goal is still thought to be important, vast new resources may be committed, as in wars or foreign aid or cancer research, on the principle that a breakthrough can be achieved only by a disproportionate increase in the scale of the means. The resource-conserving tendency appears only when the goal is not thought to be important enough for this principle to be acted upon. On the other hand, when the goal is vague enough the scale of the means employed may be set by all sorts of apparently extraneous considerations. It may be difficult to know whether the success of a particular investigation, e.g. into the structure of cells, is a step toward curing cancer. Again, the American Department of Defense does not tend to minimize its expenditure merely because sufficiency of self-defence for the United States is difficult to determine. So this second claim, when not qualified by goal-importance, seems to be empirically false. Blalock has confused the way in which a rational agent would behave, or might reasonably behave, under conditions of uncertainty, with the way in which people actually behave under such conditions. Underlying this confusion is the assumption that where the probability of success with given means is difficult to determine, people, in general, will prefer to adopt a mini-max decision principle, that is, will prefer to minimize their maximum loss. In fact, they often do not for various reasons. One, but only one, of these is that gambling with scarce resources is itself often an attractive and rational policy when the effectiveness of a more cautious one is not clear.

Much the same kind of criticism applies to Blalock's statement of the 'Flexibility Principle'. This asserts that 'Those goals that permit the least flexibility with respect to choice among alternative means can be expected to have the greatest influence in determining the direction of one's behaviour (choice behaviour), though not necessarily its intensity or persistence.' An accompanying note adds that the Principle 'is based on the assumption that individuals will act more or less rationally so as to maximize their chances of attaining all important goals. They are expected to select the most efficient means toward goals that do not permit flexibility, and then to choose means toward other goals (that do permit flexibility) according to their compatibility with the most efficient means towards the first goals.' It is also assumed that we have a goal A with few alternative means, and that one of these means is 'obviously more efficient'. Goal B has many more means, 'no one of which is clearly superior'. Some of these latter means are incompatible, but some are not incompatible, with some of the means to goal A.[1]

Under these conditions, to say that goals with the least flexible (fewest alternatives) means have a greater influence on the direction of total behaviour than do goals with more alternative means is to utter a tautology. If we are to act rationally so as to maximize our 'chances of attaining all important goals', we must—logically must—first choose the obviously efficient means to goal A, and then choose compatible means to goal B. If we reversed the order of choice, and hence the direction of influence, we should irrationally endanger our ability to achieve *both* goals, and thus should not be maximizing our chances of attaining them. All that is *meant* here by the phrase 'greater influence in determining the direction of behaviour' is 'greater restriction of alternative means'. No discovery has been made about the way in which people actually pursue goals in this world. We have only drawn out a logical implication of the phrase 'less flexible choice among means'. And this consequence will follow whether or not we have any real choices among actual means. No field work is needed, since the Flexibility Principle merely states the logical implication of certain implicit definitions and premises.

Of course, the fact that the Flexibility Principle is trivially true is not in itself a serious criticism. The question is whether the Principle has a useful part to play in Blalock's argument. The answer is that it has not. An example of its application will show this. In the chapter on 'Power and Discrimination' he writes:[2]

According to the Flexibility Principle, the possession of resources by permitting greater flexibility of choice, therefore reduces the probability that the objective or goal in question will dominate choice behaviour.
> Note: This suggests that in many situations persons who are in the best *position* to discriminate (e.g., persons who secure high statuses) may be less motivated to do so because of other available alternatives.

The claim that people in possession of resources, or of alternative means, *may* be less motivated to discriminate than people without such resources is doubly obscure. First, obscure because the phrase 'may be less motivated' is misused. The actual situation is that where there are alternative means available, people *need* not, though they may, pursue the same goal by always using the same means. The goal will not uniquely determine their choice of means. This logical

[1] *Ibid.*, pp. 48–9.   [2] *Ibid.*, p. 139.

82

consequence should not be made to resemble, as it does here, a cautious empirical statement about what the agents are likely to do if given a choice of means. We have no information about what they are likely to do, only about what it is logically open to them to do. Second, the claim is obscure because the phrase 'other available alternatives' is used ambiguously. In the formulation of the Flexibility Principle, the phrase was used to refer to alternative means to the same goal. In its application here the phrase sometimes refers to such alternative means and sometimes to alternative goals. Thus it is said that people compensate for their inability to achieve their original goals by trying to dominate the behaviour of other people. 'In terms of the notion of alternative means, they are attempting to find some reasonably satisfactory alternative. In the process, the original objective may become lost and the need to dominate may become the overwhelming obsession.'[1] When this happens, however, the original Flexibility Principle no longer applies, since our increased flexibility of choice now amounts to choice among different goals rather than choice of different means to the same goal. Yet we cannot rephrase the Principle so as to legitimate this ambiguity. For if we did so we should make completely empty the assertion that 'the possession of resources, by permitting greater flexibility of choice, therefore reduces the probability that the objective or goal in question will dominate choice behaviour.'

2. Blalock's theoretical propositions: tautological or false?

It may be replied that the very name of the Flexibility Principle suggests that its author does not take it for an empirical assertion, and that while it may be useless it is also harmless. 'Therefore', the reply may continue, 'if we are to find fault with Blalock's list of theoretical propositions we shall have to look at additional candidates whose claims to be empirical hypotheses are more straightforward.' So let us now do that. We can begin with one listed immediately after the Flexibility Principle. It is put thus:[2]

> Economic and status factors are most likely to be major determinants of minority discrimination if *both* of the following hold: (a) there are a relatively small number of means to status and economic goals that are perceived to be efficient; and (b) discriminatory behaviour is perceived to be instrumental, either for large numbers of persons or for influential elites, in achieving status objectives by these most efficient means.

What this proposition asserts about economic and status goals is

---

[1] *Ibid.*, p. 116. [2] *Ibid.*, p. 49.

not quite clear. It *seems* to assert that they will exercise a major attraction if the efficient means appear, to the agents, to be limited in number, 'and discriminatory behaviour is perceived to be instrumental' in the use of these means. But the problem is to clarify the relation between these means and discrimination. We are not told whether discriminatory behaviour is *itself* one of those efficient means, as far as the agents are concerned, or whether such behaviour is merely a means to those efficient means. The difference is of practical importance. For if the only way that I can join the golf club of my dreams is by owning a house in a particular neighbourhood, then as a means to *that* means, I may have to advocate a policy of discrimination in order to be admitted to that neighbourhood. This is different from the case in which, as a matter of policy, only known and practising discriminators within the neighbourhood are admitted to membership in the club. The difference is important here for the following reason.

If discrimination itself is supposed to be a direct means to the goal, then the whole proposition is obviously non-empirical. It is entailed by—follows from the sense of—the phrase 'a rational goal-seeking agent', an agent, that is, who chooses one of the means he takes to be efficient. For as we have just seen, the Flexibility Principle which is being applied here assumes 'that individuals will act more or less rationally so as to maximize their chances of attaining all important goals.' Here again, it is wrong to say that 'economic and status factors are *most likely* to be major determinants of minority discrimination.' As one of a small number of means to such goals, discriminatory behaviour will be either equi-probable with the other available means, or not. If not, then some empirical factor will produce the difference. This factor will need to be described, and the description incorporated into the original hypothesis. In either case, the present use of the phrase 'most likely' is incorrect.

On the other hand, if discrimination is only a means to a means, then everything depends on whether it is one of a very limited number of such secondary means. For if there are many, even the most rational agent need not choose discrimination. And if he does not, the proposition is false. So there must be very few secondary means. But then the proposition is trivially true. It merely says that a rational agent will be likely to use discriminatory means when there are few alternative means to the goals which he pursues. Hence the proposition is either plainly false or obviously analytic. In neither event will it qualify as being a plausible candidate for the role of scientific hypothesis.

The next proposition on Blalock's list presents rather similar difficulties. It reads:[1]

[1] *Ibid.*, p. 49.

In comparing individuals with respect to discriminatory behaviour, those persons who are least able to achieve status goals through means not involving discrimination are most likely to be motivated to discriminate. Since these persons may lack the resources to carry out the discrimination, however, it does not follow that actual discrimination will be more pronounced in the case of such individuals.

This asserts that the *rational* agents who have the least choice in avoiding discriminatory means will be those who are also 'most likely to be *motivated* to discriminate'. The crucial question here is how the words 'to be *motivated*' are to be interpreted. They may mean 'have the best reason'. If so, the proposition is analytic, since the rational agent with the fewest ways of avoiding discrimination will have, as a matter of logic, the best reason for using discrimination as a means toward his goal—always assuming that he has no countervailing reasons. Again, the words may mean 'to be tempted'. If they do, we must then distinguish three different points about temptations. The first is that in one sense of 'tempt' we are tempted whenever we are *offered* an opportunity. The second is that in another sense of 'tempt' we are tempted only if we are *inclined*, however briefly, to *accept* the opportunity. The third point is that we may or may not *actually succumb* to a temptation. Even if we do not, we still may have been tempted to do so in the first two senses of the word. Or the temptation may have been put before us as an opportunity which held no attraction; and so we may have been tempted only in the first sense, that of having been given an opportunity.

Hence, 'being motivated to discriminate' may mean: (1) 'offered an opportunity and succumbed', (2) 'offered an opportunity and did not succumb', (3) 'offered an opportunity and was inclined to succumb but did not', (4) 'offered an opportunity and was not even inclined to succumb, and so did not'. Which of these is appropriate here? It makes a difference. Were the agents most likely to succumb? Or most likely to be merely inclined to succumb without actually doing so? Or most likely to be not even so inclined? If it is the second alternative of this last triad, as the full quotation suggests, then we are given no reason for believing that the agents were *inclined* to succumb though they did not. No reason, that is, unless the proposition is taken to be analytically true. For the people who are least able to achieve status goals by non-discriminatory means must be, it follows logically, those who will be also most inclined to succumb to discriminatory means. Those means are the only ones left if the original goals are to be pursued.

The following proposition is drawn from the same set as the others.

Despite its length, it merely asserts that the most disliked and helpless identifiable minority is identical with the one most likely to attract the displaced aggression of the majority.[1]

> A minority that deviates from important group norms is especially likely to become a target for displaced aggression to the degree that: (a) the deviance increases the visibility of the minority; (b) the deviance is itself a frustration to members of the dominant group; (c) the deviance contributes a threat to sacred traditions; (d) the deviance makes it easier to rationalize aggression, thereby reducing the amount of guilt or self-punishment; and (e) the deviance leaves the minority unprotected by the larger society and therefore vulnerable to aggression.

Clearly, the target group is not especially vulnerable to *displaced* aggression; any aggression will serve, whether or not it arises from frustration. Now put in this way, it is by no means certain that the proposition is true, and more important, even testable. For suppose the majority miscalculates, and the minority they attack is not really the most visible, available, and vulnerable. Suppose there is another group which is even more disliked and helpless, though not attacked. Is this supposition allowable? Whichever answer we give, there is the same difficulty. How can we define the helplessness, or lack of protection, of the minority independently of its being attacked? We seem to know which group is the most helpless or vulnerable only by finding out which group is most successfully attacked. If a group were to appear vulnerable but was not in fact assaulted, we could always produce the explanation that it was protected by the aggressor's fear of guilt feelings. But if we did, it would become an analytic truth that the most helpless and vulnerable minority is identical with the one most likely to be attacked.

> If there are two parties, one dominant and the other subordinate, the fewer the resources of the subordinate party, and the fewer its realistic alternatives, the greater is the number of alternatives available to the dominant party in controlling the behaviour of the subordinate party.

This proposition[2] is only a step away, if that, from being tautologous. It says that the fewer the feasible alternatives open to a subordinate party, the greater are the number open to the dominant party in controlling the other one. This is merely a special case of the Flexibility Principle already discussed: that given certain assumptions, the fewer moves are open to one player in a competitive (zero-sum) game, the more are open to his opponent. It is given

[1] *Ibid.*, pp. 49–50.   [2] *Ibid.*, p. 50.

that one party is dominant; so the weaker the dominated party—the fewer its resources and alternatives—the stronger the dominant party *must* be. This conclusion, again, is one of logic and not of experience.

The last two propositions to be brought forward as examples are about slavery. The first reads thus:[1]

> Where resources are closed to the subordinate party (i.e., where subsistence is not easily acquired and is dependent on the possession of substantial capital), a system of tenancy or contract labor will be preferable (for the dominant party) to one of slavery or serfdom. Slavery and serfdom are therefore more likely to be found in situations in which resources are open, and where labor can be retained only by applying direct force or political controls implying the threat of force.

The second sentence of this quotation states that slavery and serfdom will be more likely to occur where they are the only means available for retaining the desired labour force. This claim raises several questions of interest. How do we know that these are the *only* available means, given the situation? Presumably, because we know enough about that situation to realize that unless slavery or serfdom are employed the society will have to change in difficult and important respects. Perhaps a system of costly incentives will have to be used, and who will pay for that? So the assumption is that slavery and serfdom are the only available means for retaining a labour force, given that the society is to remain unchanged in other important respects, e.g. if it is to continue to meet the growing economic demands of a political élite. However, if we know *this* much about a society it must already have been functioning for some time; otherwise, we could not be worried about its remaining unchanged.

Therefore our proposition becomes this: 'Slavery and serfdom will be more likely to occur where they are the only means of retaining labour that do not require the functioning society in question to change in other important respects, whatever these may be.' When we now ask what these important respects can be, the answer can be given only as 'whatever the society is less prepared to change than it is *not* to employ slavery, assuming the choice to lie between them.' If we substitute this answer in our proposition we obtain: 'Slavery and serfdom will be more likely to occur where they are the only means of retaining labour that do not require the functioning society in question to change in a way which it is less prepared to do than not using slaves.' But this simply says that slavery will be more likely to occur if it is the only means that does not require the society to change in a way that it is less prepared to do than not to use

[1] *Ibid.*

slaves. And this is a tautology. If slavery is, in the circumstances, the only means of avoiding a change, a change which is rejected in favour of slavery, then slavery will most certainly occur and there is no 'more likely' about it. The formulation of the original claim merely conceals its triviality.

On the other hand, the second proposition about slavery is not quite so empty.[1]

> If resources are open and slavery profitable, it is usually easier to control slaves by force if (i) they are not members of indigenous groups, (ii) they have been transported from long distances, and (iii) they have diverse cultural backgrounds. This is especially true if: (a) geographic conditions are such that escape is relatively easy and where indigenous slaves could not easily be distinguished from local peasants or other elements of the population; (b) linguistic differences or tribal rivalries inhibit effective slave revolts or other forms of protest; (c) it is feasible or necessary to treat slaves harshly, either because the supply is plentiful or because it is economically rational to do so.

This proposition claims that forcible control of slaves is usually easier if the various resources which enable them to resist are diminished. The claim is not quite empty, for the diminution of the slaves' resources is itemized: the slaves are foreign, transported, and culturally diverse. What this itemization does is to remind—or sometimes inform—us of the type of resistance resources. More important, however, is the fact that the proposition suffers from the inclusion of the words 'it is usually easier to control'. For if we wish to list the factors which diminish resistance, we must be careful to take these factors as doing no more than serving as *illustrations* of the sort of thing which usually makes slaves easier to control. Once factors like being foreign, transported, and culturally diverse have been itemized, we must not then think that we have produced a law-like statement which correlates their presence with that of the forcible control of slaves.

Yet this is the danger to which the phrasing of our proposition exposes us. The reason is that there are indefinitely many conditions whose presence make forcible control of slaves easier: for example, their being non-suicidal and non-homicidal, their being afraid of physical punishment. Why should we fasten upon some of these rather than on others? It may well be true that if the ones mentioned are present then slave control is easier. But it will be true, also, that the presence of some of those not listed would make control easier.

Compare our present proposition with the statement that a pint of water freezes if placed in a butcher's meat freezer, and also if left

[1] *Ibid.*, pp. 50–1.

outdoors in winter snow at night. Both these conditions under which water freezes embody a common factor. We now characterize it as 'exposure to temperature of 0°C for a variable but specifiable length of time'. This factor had, at one time, to be discovered, and simple generalizations produced about the freezing point of water and the rate at which conversion into ice takes place. Our present proposition has not yet reached that stage of generalization. The proposition merely enumerates various conditions under which some unknown factors are thought to operate so as to ensure that slave-control is likely to be easier. However, to list these conditions is simply to list the kinds of local, or *initial*, conditions under which some unknown law-like generalization is thought to hold. And doing this is clearly different from providing us with the generalization itself.

The same remark applies to one of our earlier propositions, the proposition which states that the most disliked and helpless identifiable minority is the one most likely to attract the displaced aggression of the majority. The kinds of conditions specified in the statement—the visibility and vulnerability of the minority, its role as a frustration and threat to the majority—form only a small sample of the indefinitely large number of sorts of conditions which might be given. In fact, two of these sorts are listed in a proposition immediately preceding the present one. That previous proposition says 'minorities are likely to be selected as targets for aggression to the degree that such aggression can serve as a means to *other* goals'. Thus aggression can serve both to handicap minority competitors and to make them more pliable.[1]

Of course, once we produce a well-formed universal hypothesis, we then are able to identify the kinds of local, or initial, conditions under which it operates. For they are simply the conditions which satisfy, either directly or indirectly, the requirements described in the antecedent clause of the hypothesis. For example, in the generalization 'If the temperature is 0°C or lower for a specifiable length of time, then water exposed in it under normal atmospheric pressure will freeze', the conditions which satisfy the temperature requirement are ones like: being in a butcher's meat freezer and being left outdoors at night in Enderby Land. Here we know what to look for: exposure for a certain length of time to a temperature which falls within a particular range (0°C or below). But the two propositions about minorities and the control of slaves respectively are not in this happy situation. In each of them we have yet to discover what common factors, if any, the listed conditions embody. And the danger in each such case is that we shall take the members of our list as jointly forming either a causally necessary or a causally sufficient or a causally necessary and sufficient condition of the events referred

[1] *Ibid.*, p. 49.

to in the apodosis. Yet here we can be fairly sure that the members of our lists do not jointly form either a causally necessary or a causally sufficient and necessary condition. If the members did, we should not be able to lengthen the lists at will, as we can, and so reveal that the lists do not supply us with all the conditions necessary for producing the effects.

To this criticism someone may reply that while the conditions taken jointly are neither causally necessary nor necessary and sufficient, they nevertheless are sufficient. For example, it is sufficient for easier control of slaves by force that they be identifiable, find it hard to escape, and hard to unite. This statement, then, is a universal hypothesis and not simply a statement about the kinds of situations in which an unknown generalization holds.

However, this reply raises familiar difficulties. What do we mean here by 'easier control of slaves by force'? We mean that their control gives us less effort, worry, and discomfort than would be the case if all relevant conditions but these three remained the same. For if we allowed some of those other conditions to vary also, we should have to take account of the effect on our claim of new, and possibly disturbing, factors. But if other relevant conditions remain unchanged, the causal sufficiency of our three conditions is suspect. It is suspect because taken at their face value the conditions are not jointly sufficient for easier control of slaves by force. If all the slaves are either homicidal or suicidal or both, as many slaves once were, then their being non-indigenous, transported, and culturally diverse will not be sufficient to make them usually easier to control by force. They will kill and be done with it. Similarly, if they are unafraid of pain, their inability to combine or escape may be outweighed by their capacity to endure punishment and worry their masters.

On the other hand, if the three conditions are given a stronger interpretation, we run the danger of having them logically imply easier control, and hence of having them become not a causally sufficient but a *logically* sufficient condition. In this case we should escape, also, from the problem of supplying causally necessary conditions—at the cost of giving up the search for an empirical hypothesis. That the cost amounts to this is clear if, first, we interpret the three conditions as recognizability, friendlessness, and disorganization; and, second, we rule out, as causally inoperative, such counteracting factors as fearlessness and homicidal tendencies. For then the result is that increased recognizability and friendlessness and disorganization logically imply, singly and jointly, increased ease of control by force. Within the situation contemplated, it would be self-contradictory to assert that increased ease of slave-recognition or increased disorganization or friendlessness among slaves did not make their physical control easier. The former would be examples of what is referred to by the very meaning of the phrase 'increased ease of physical control': that we can recognize the slaves more easily, that they have fewer helpful local friends, that they help each other against us less than they did before.

In general, then, the 'theoretical propositions' offered by Blalock display the familiar uneasy oscillation between falsity and triviality complained of by critics of sociological hypotheses. The question is why this oscillation should occur so commonly. In a narrow but uninteresting sense, the answer has already been given. It is that, at best, the so-called hypotheses enumerate the initial conditions under which some unknown law-like generalizations are presumed to be operating. These initial conditions, taken jointly, are mistaken for the antecedents of universal hypotheses, a mistake which can be defended from obvious criticism only by strengthening the initial conditions so that they logically entail the consequent. But this renders the statement analytic, and hence useless as a candidate for the role of empirical hypothesis. At worst, of course, even this oscillation is absent. The supposed hypothesis is undisguisedly analytic, as in the proposition, previously discussed, which asserts that the fewer the feasible alternatives open to a subordinate party, the greater the number open to the dominant party in controlling the other one. Here the question to be answered is why this analytic proposition should ever be taken for an empirical one, since its falsity is an obvious logical impossibility.

3. The notion of a social law

Discussions about the nature of scientific laws have revolved around these three issues:

(1) the difference between accidental generalizations and nomological generalizations (laws);

(2) the difference between empirical (or non-theoretical) laws and theoretical laws;

(3) the difference between universal laws and probabilistic (or statistical) laws.

Each of these distinctions raises many well-known and far-reaching problems into which we need not enter. Our task here is much simpler. We only need to characterize the relationship of social laws to scientific laws in general; and the simplest way of doing this is in terms of the three distinctions listed above. For taken jointly, they indicate the features which all scientific laws, including social laws, must have if they are to perform the work allotted to them by scientists.

The distinction between accidental and nomological generalizations is more easily shown and referred to than accounted for: 'All

Australian prime ministers are male', 'All the books in my room are octavo size', 'All industrial societies are monogamous' are undoubtedly examples of accidental generalizations. Similarly, 'All pure water boils at 100°C at sea level', 'The boiling point of a liquid is raised whenever a solid is dissolved in it', 'At a given temperature the absolute pressure and volume of a gas vary inversely', are examples, commonly given, of simple physical laws. What such laws share with accidental generalizations is their basic logical form. Both are universal conditional statements, so that 'All A are B' is to be read as 'For every x, if x is A then x is B'. Such statement-forms assert that if certain events occur, or if certain states or objects exist, then certain other events also occur, or certain other states and objects also exist. Universal conditional statements, then, assert a uniform connection or relationship between objects or states or events or situations but do not assert their existence. Such statements merely claim that if and when conditions of sort S occur, then conditions of type T also occur. In the case of a social generalization, for example, conditions S may be found in few societies, times, and places.

What most obviously distinguishes accidental from nomological generalizations is that the latter support, while the former do not support, subjunctive and counterfactual conditional statements. A subjunctive conditional like 'If this piece of solid salt should be dissolved in this pot of heated water, then the boiling point of the water would be raised' is supported or justified by reference, first, to the law about dissolved solids increasing the boiling point of a liquid, and second, to statements of initial conditions which ensure that the law is applicable to this particular case. The same sort of support is given to a counterfactual subjunctive like 'If this piece of solid salt had been dissolved in this pot of water—though in fact it was not—the boiling point of the water would have been raised'. Nomological generalizations authorize us to draw inferences about cases that do not now occur, have not occurred in the past, and may not or will not occur in the future. That a law has no actual instances, or will never have any, does not in itself prevent the law from holding. For the law asserts a hypothetical relationship, an invariable connection, whether or not the relationship is actually exemplified.

The situation with respect to accidental generalizations is quite different. They are not interpreted as making any claims about potential cases, subjunctive or counterfactual. The generalization that all the books in my room now are octavo in size does not justify the assertion that any additional book put in my room will be octavo in size. Nor does the fact that until now all Australian prime ministers have been men support the claim that every Australian prime minister will be, or must be, male. Even if such accidental generalizations turn out always to hold in fact, at all times and places, this will be a happy accident and not a consequence of there being a law-like connection between the properties in question or, more basically, of there being a scientific theory from which the generalization can be derived. There seems to be no scientific theory which would preclude a woman from being a prime minister of Australia, and so the fact that no woman has yet filled that post does not seem to support the generalization that the post can be, and must be, filled only by a man. The truth of 'All Australian prime ministers are male' is the result of the historical development of local practice and not of scientific necessity.

But even if there were a law or constitutional provision in Australia which precluded women from becoming prime minister, this legal rule would not, of course, be a nomological generalization. At best, the law would state what had become a local social practice. However, even universal statements of social practices which are everywhere rigidly adhered to do not qualify as social laws for that reason alone. Only if the statement of the practice either (a) is supported by an accepted social law or by a set of inter-related social laws—an accepted social theory—or (b) does not bar certain hypothetical cases which an accepted law or theory admits as possible, will the universal statement of the social practice be a suitable candidate as a statement of a social law. Most statements of social practices meet neither of these conditions. Not only are most statements of social practices not phrased as universal conditionals, but when they are, these statements are seldom supported by an accepted law or theory, whether social, psychological, or physical; and most universal statements of social practices *do* bar hypothetical cases which are admitted by such laws and theories. Thus the universal generalization 'All industrial societies are monogamous' is neither supported by an accepted law nor does the statement admit the hypothetical case of a polyandrous industrial society. Yet no accepted law rules out such a case.

The question whether there is a useful *general* distinction to be drawn between empirical and theoretical laws has been much debated. It is not, however, a question which we need to answer here. For we are concerned here only with the possibility, and usefulness, of distinguishing in specific situations, and for specific purposes, between empirical and theoretical social laws. The importance, for us, of being clear about the distinction is simply this: sociologists often confuse accidental universal generalizations with *empirical* universal generalizations. The confusion arises for sociologists because their generalizations are so commonly based on, or derived from, observational considerations rather than theoretical ones. Both sorts—accidental and empirical—are sociological

93

generalizations from observed regularities, and the question whether a given generalization is merely accidental or is a genuine law need not have a ready answer. For we may not know whether a given generalization is supported by accepted laws and theories, or we may not be able to determine, with any ease, whether it bars hypothetical cases not ruled out by accepted laws and theories. In consequence, some universal statements of social practice may be taken to be empirical generalizations (observational laws) when they may be only accidental generalizations. An example—one to which we shall return later—is: 'In all societies there are incest taboos.'

This difficulty is not so serious in the case of theoretical laws. Since they are not generalizations based on observed regularities, there is no temptation to mistake a class of known observed cases for a class of possible observable ones. A theoretical law, in distinction to an empirical law, contains descriptive terms which do not appear in the statements used to test it. These terms do not have independent operational specifications—operations which are independent of whatever meaning the terms derive from the theoretical law itself. That is, theoretical laws contain, as empirical laws do not, terms which have no direct operational or experimental procedures for their use. Their sense is given implicitly, or indirectly, by the basic vocabulary, claims, and uses of the theory to which the theoretical terms belong. They presuppose the theoretical law in a way in which the descriptive terms of an empirical law do not presuppose the law in which they occur. Because this is so, a theoretical law is not open to *direct* test by observed instances whereas the scope of an empirical law does essentially include such direct experimental cases. In fact, it is a distinguishing feature of an empirical law, as against a theoretical one, that it can be established by direct instances, even though what will count as a direct instance or an observable case is very much dependent on how the distinction between observation and theory is drawn in a particular context. For what count as observation statements in one context presuppose the truth of what count as theoretical laws in another context.

Thus the weak development in sociology of useful theoretical laws, and the theories of which they are a part, has two effects upon the development of empirical laws. First, the comparative absence of theoretical laws makes it difficult to distinguish empirical laws from accidental generalizations, since we cannot use either theoretical support or subjunctive difference as tests for separating them. Second, the scarcity of theoretical laws results in a lack of systematic connection among the empirical generalizations which sociologists have managed to advance or establish independently of theoretical considerations. But even a large collection of independent empirical laws can be used to explain and predict only restricted classes of qualitatively similar occurrences or situations. The explanatory scope of such independent laws is narrow because, for one, the use of their descriptive terms is closely set by operational procedures which are independently specifiable. Only theories—which are not so restricted —can relate empirical generalizations in such a way that the qualitatively diverse ranges of events to which they refer can be given a common explanation. Yet unless this can be done we have no reliable apparatus for generating proposals for new empirical generalizations. Nor have we, except in the most primitive sense, a science of sociology rather than a mere natural history of social life.

The third important distinction is that between universal and probabilistic (or statistical) laws. Its chief practical interest for sociologists comes from the problem of inferring a probabilistic causal relationship from a correlation of variables. A probabilistic law has the form $p(A,B)=r$, that is, the probability for a case of property B to be a case of property A is r, where r is the long term, but otherwise unspecified, relative frequency with which events of class A tend to appear, given reference class B. (A correlation between two measured variables is sometimes a statement of the relative frequency—though not the long-term relative frequency— with which instances of a given property have been found to be instances of another specific property). But since the explanatory value of a correlation largely depends on our being able to rely on its holding for unexamined populations, the question constantly arises whether a particular correlation can be so relied upon, and if so whether it may not reveal a causal connection, or even express a probabilistic law. Because the investigator has a legitimately vested interest in extending the applicability of his correlation as far as possible, the temptation for him to forget about causally important restrictions on his original variables is always present when he applies the correlation to new groups. This is particularly easy, as we have seen, if the original variables were so loosely defined that the nature of their constraints is open to debate.

The most obvious important difference between universal laws (or strictly universal statements) and statistical laws is that from the latter nothing follows about any given instance, or any finite set of instances, of the reference class. In $p(A,B)=r$, any particular case of property B may or may not actually turn out to be a case of property A; r simply indicates the proportion which is highly likely to appear in the long run. For this reason the use of statistical laws in explanation or prediction cannot give a deductive conclusion but only an inductive one; the premises may strongly support, but cannot, in contrast to universal laws, logically imply the conclusion. Hence, the explanation or prediction of any given case is much weaker when a statistical law is used than when a universal law is available. However, the two kinds of laws are similar in that both support subjunctive and counterfactual statements, though these, when supported by a statistical law, must themselves be statistical and state the probability which holds for the hypothetical case.

On the other hand, the testing of probabilistic laws is much more complex and difficult than is the testing of universal laws. We have to formulate rules for accepting or rejecting statistical hypotheses according to how closely the long-term relative frequencies of their observed outcomes fit the predicted outcomes. But the closeness of fit demanded will depend upon how much value we attach, in a given instance, to the avoidance of (a) failing to accept a correct statistical hypothesis, and (b) accepting an incorrect one. In turn, the importance we place upon avoiding these errors in a particular instance will be determined by a host of practical and theoretical considerations: that is, by the practical and theoretical benefits which can reasonably be expected to come from accepting the hypothesis if it is true and of rejecting it if it is false.

Statistical generalization, whether law-like or not, has a special interest for the sociologist, for that is the form which most of his general empirical claims take. They are either accidental generalizations expressing correlations based on examined populations or they are statements of a nomological and probabilistic kind, although the latter may not be stated numerically. In so far as we have empirical, as against theoretical, social laws they are—and are likely to continue to be—statistical ones. The reason has been given by Ernest Nagel. It is that the sorts of questions which we usually ask about social issues like discrimination, poverty, status, and class arise from ordinary social activities described in our everyday and technically unrefined vocabulary. These common-sense terms usually refer to classes of non-homogeneous items, and the generalizations which we discover to hold between such diversely populated classes are inevitably probabilistic rather than universal. Moreover, if we attempted to refine our terms there might be no real gain. For our everyday terms mark out the social behaviour which is of practical importance to us; and it is this behaviour which sets the sociological problems that chiefly interest the investigator. If we altered our descriptive vocabulary, and hence our concepts, we might obtain universal generalization at the cost of transforming, and thus losing, the very problems which we began by trying to solve. Rough statistical generalizations may be the best which our preferred questions about social affairs permit. Further refinement of vocabulary and generalization may simply take us far beyond the requirements of the problems which concern us most.[1] This point emphasizes, once again, the close

[1] See *The Structure of Science*, London, 1961, pp. 505–8.

connection between problem characterization, the operational specifications of terms, and the adequacy of generalizations.

Once we ask the vague question 'What kinds of social laws might
sociologists be able to find?' we soon come to realize how many
different kinds there might be. There might be, for example, empirical
universal laws, empirical probabilistic laws, theoretical universal
laws, and theoretical probabilistic laws. There might be laws, as we
shall see, concerning individual actors and laws about groups; there
might also be laws about both. There could be non-causal laws
expressing an invariable concomitance of certain properties; or
sequential causal laws concerning certain kinds of events, properties,
or situations. The subjects of all these laws could range very widely:
some of the laws might state causal connections between types of
social organization and aspects of the natural environment, such as
climate, fauna, flora, and soils; some laws might correlate social
change with technological innovation or with the rise of new types
of personality or with new forms of economic institutions; still other
laws might connect different kinds of social organization in different
societies with the same psychological needs and demands. All of the
preceding might or might not be expressible as mathematical functions; and these functions might state the concurrent variation over
time of two or more measurable properties, or of two or more sets
of complex properties having the form of processes. In brief,
sociologists might be able to find any of the familiar types of scientific
law. But the kinds of law statements that sociologists actually formulate will be determined by the kinds of problems for which answers
are sought. If the problems are wide in scope, phrased in common-
sense terms, and bound by the needs of a particular social policy,
then the generalizations applicable to those problems will be
correspondingly wide-ranging, imprecise, and statistical. If the problems are highly specific, described with technical precision, and
theoretically directed, they will permit, though not necessitate, the
formulation of generalizations with those qualities. We cannot,
however, retain our everyday social problems and expect to find
precise and powerful generalizations to apply to them, any more
than we can expect to find such generalizations in physics by
restricting ourselves to questions like 'How much longer (on the
average) will an asphalt road last without maintenance than a
gravel one?'

4. Social rules, causal laws, and 'quasi-laws'

In the wider and more interesting sense, then, the problem of accounting for the sociologists' dilemma remains to be solved. But a clue
to the solution lies in this fact: social scientists have often confused

the search for laws concerning various kinds of rule-guided, or rule-governed, behaviour with the search for a quite different kind of generalization: that supposed to guide, or govern, behaviour by means of law-like causal rules. The latter search is the product of confusion, the former is reasonable. For even the most general rules—ones which make no essential reference to particular agents, places or times—do not and cannot have the status of causal laws that 'guide', or 'govern', the agents' behaviour. The behaviour in which sociologists are professionally interested is characteristically, but by no means exclusively, rule-guided, or at least rule-making and rule-breaking. Thus we can often explain an agent's action in terms of a rule which he is observing or not observing, or in terms of a rule which his behaviour is helping to establish. The social regularities of behaviour in which rules are put into practice, or fail to be put into practice, however, are part of what we wish to explain by means of social laws. The social regularities of behaviour are not themselves exemplifications of such laws, though the fact that a certain rule is either adhered or not adhered to by certain people under certain conditions may be an instance of the operation of a social law.

Hence it is important to distinguish genuine social laws from social rules, and to distinguish both from the social regularities of behaviour, thought, and attitude which are the putting into practice of social rules and which are evidence for the latter's presence. Just as there are different kinds of rules, there are different kinds of rule-following. All rules pick out, either for all people or a specified class of people, a set of performances which are demanded, allowed, or prohibited. Rules include, on the one hand, explicit regulations which are formally introduced, altered, and enforced, and on the other hand, implicit and unstated prudential or moral precepts which are absorbed by imitation, often unconsciously, and maintained by informal, and sometimes unsuspected, social pressure. Between these two extremes lie such rules as are represented by instructions of various sorts, rules of thumb, or those displayed in loosely organized forms of play, and in clearly defined but not legally obligatory status and role behaviour.[1] Rules resemble genuine social laws in that both can always be put into words; again, both may, but need not be, exemplified by any existing situation, for there are neglected rules and counterfactual laws. Unlike any law, however, some rules can be introduced, changed or withdrawn at will, enforced, obeyed or violated. Two existing rules can be incompatible whereas two laws cannot both hold. Rules can be made and developed, laws must be discovered. There may be social laws con-

[1] These remarks about rules owe much to Max Black's paper, 'The Analysis of Rules', reprinted in *Models and Metaphors*, Ithaca, New York, 1962, pp. 95–139.

cerning the conditions under which certain kinds of social rules arise, but there are no rules laying down the conditions under which social laws must be discovered.

These features of rules have their counterpart in certain features of rule-following behaviour. Rules can be followed whole-heartedly or reluctantly, professedly or actually, by most people or few, wittingly or unwittingly, seldom or constantly by a given person. Rules differ greatly in the amount and kind of constraint they place upon the rule-follower. Adhering to the rules of games like tennis and bridge, or the norms of the occupational role of surgeon, is quite different from obeying the rules of a prison barracks, a naval ship, or a geriatric ward in a hospital. The rules of a game are followed with pleasure by the players because they wish to play that game; the rules of a professional role are adhered to voluntarily; but the disciplinary rules of a prison camp are followed by the inmates because they do not wish to be punished. The inmates' own informal rules are followed for still different reasons. Games embrace only a small part of most peoples' lives, occupational roles a larger part. Total institutions, however—prisons, hospitals, army camps, convents, geriatric homes—produce total roles which embrace, constrain, and structure all aspects of a person's life. His behaviour can be very largely explained in terms of his membership in such an institution and its causal effects upon him.

Rule-following commonly, but not always, results in regular behaviour, and in the case of social groups, in social regularities. But if some of the rules that are being followed turn out to be logically incompatible, then no regular behaviour *need* ensue. A similar result may occur if the rule being adhered to is internally inconsistent. When regularities of behaviour do result from rule-following, it is often necessary to distinguish between those regularities which are the embodiment of the rule and those regularities which are intended, or natural, consequences of the former, or are its unintended effects, although themselves neither causal nor rule-governed. Regularities of rule-exemplification, and regularities that are the desired, expected, or usual consequences of such exemplification, are sometimes brought together indiscriminately under the heading 'regularities of rule-following behaviour'. But the regularity of behaviour which consists in people obeying the municipal ordinance not to smoke in theatres may have all sorts of distinct, though regular, behavioural consequences, expected and desired (tobacco sales at adjoining shops never rise above a certain level), and unexpected and unwanted (the incidence of domestic quarrels among the town's residents increases, for heavy smokers stay at home). These three regularities are quite different in type and content.

The value of distinguishing them can be illustrated by noticing the confusion into which neglect of their differences is likely to lead us. Helmer and Rescher, for example, think that in the social sciences there is a class of well-confirmed, loosely law-like statements which they call 'historical laws'. These describe 'the actions of an organized group of men under certain restrictive conditions'. Some instances of these laws are: 'A census takes place in the U.S. in every decade year', 'Heretics were persecuted in seventeenth-century Spain', 'In the sea fights of sailing vessels in the period 1653–1803, large formations were too cumbersome for effectual control as single units'.[1] Such 'quasi-laws' do not, it is claimed, merely summarize a number of singular statements about actual instances. Quasi-laws account for new cases and have counterfactual force. The known cases simply 'provide a part of the appropriate evidence for the historical generalization'.[2]

Quasi-laws are loose, then, in that they are either explicitly or implicitly conditional in form; but the conditions referred to, or assumed, cannot be described with any precision or completeness. In consequence, these laws have exceptions, for the laws tell us what happens 'as a rule'. Exceptions are shown not to meet some 'appropriate (if hitherto unformulated) condition of the law's applicability'.[3] As an example, Helmer and Rescher cite the case of Jean Bart who is an apparent exception to the historical law that in France before the Revolution only the sons of noblemen were given naval commissions. The case shows us, they suggest, how this quasi-law has attached to it an implicit *ceteris paribus* clause stating 'unless the regulation was explicitly waived or an oversight or fraud occurred or some other similarly exceptional condition obtained'.[4] Such a clause also distinguishes quasi-laws from statistical laws. 'For a statistical law asserts the presence of some characteristic in a certain (presumably high) percentage of cases, whereas a quasi-law asserts it in all cases for which an exceptional status (in some ill-defined but clearly understood sense) cannot be claimed.'[5]

From this account of quasi-laws it is clear that they are in no sense laws. The examples given are the putting into practice of social rules, or are social regularities and practices, and their causal consequences. The looseness which these display—their proneness to exceptions—is simply due to the fact that social rules and practices are not invariably followed; thus the causal consequences of such rule-following behaviour do not invariably occur. The reason that

---

[1] O. Helmer and N. Rescher, 'Exact or Inexact Sciences: A More Instructive Dichotomy?', reprinted in *The Nature and Scope of Social Science*, ed. L. I. Krimerman, New York, 1969, p. 183.
[2] *Ibid.*   [3] *Ibid.*, p. 184.
[4] *Ibid.*   [5] *Ibid.*, p. 186.

quasi-laws are dependent on background conditions which cannot be stated precisely and completely is to be explained in the same way. We have no assurance that a particular group of people will continue to adhere to their previous practices because, *ex hypothesi*, we do not know the conditions on which those practices causally depend. All we can do, in the circumstances, is to indicate some of the other regularities and factors that seem to affect the existence of the practices in question.

The supposed explanatory ability and counterfactual force of quasi-laws is attributable to their rule-like, not to their law-like, character. The institutional practice referred to in the statement 'A census takes place in the U.S. in every decade year' depends chiefly on the pleasure of the Bureau of Census and the U.S. Congress. Changes in the U.S. census intervals often are discussed, and unless we have grounds for thinking that such changes are very unlikely to be adopted, we have no reason for relying on ten-year intervals in the future. The statement has no explanatory or counterfactual force of its own; for that force to hold we must have good reason to think that the practice will continue. Otherwise, the statement is a mere description of what has happened to date.

The case of persecution of heretics in seventeenth-century Spain is no different. The statement 'Heretics were persecuted in seventeenth-century Spain' has an exact parallel in 'Jews were not admitted to membership in the Melbourne Club in the year 1970.' The reason why we are entitled to infer, counterfactually, that if Rabbi Goldman had applied for membership in 1970 he would not have been elected, is obvious. The Melbourne Club in 1970 had a covert policy of excluding known Jews. If there were no such policy or practice, we should have no grounds for believing that Rabbi Goldman would not be elected merely because he was a Jew. The absence of new Jewish members in 1970 would be no bar to our thinking that if a qualified Jew had applied he would have been admitted. Similarly, if Mrs Jones, our neighbour, had been a heretic in seventeenth-century Spain we should expect her to be persecuted because we know this was the policy in practice. If there had been no such practice, no such rule-guided behaviour, the persecution might have been due to accidentally associated factors like popular hatred of the red hair which all heretics happened to have. But this hatred would be no reason for us now to claim that Mrs Jones, a brunette, would have been persecuted if she had been a heretic then.

The taking of the U.S. Census every decade is the outcome of an institutional regulation and the persecution of heretics in seventeenth-century Spain the result of a theocratic policy. The ineffective control of large fighting fleets in the period 1653–1803, however, is somewhat different. It is the causal result of the technological limitation on armament, ships, and communications of that period, given certain tactics and strategies. The inadequacy of the means available for carrying out these tactics and strategies produced ineffective control of long battle-lines of ships. The statement which refers to this outcome is derivable from (1) a very large set of physical and physiological laws taken in conjunction with (2) a set of statements that describe the initial conditions of the period 1653–1803, including the relevant tactics and strategies. Like all technological statements, this one depends for its explanatory force on the laws from which it is derived. In this respect it resembles 'You can't drive a tenpenny nail into a concrete wall with your bare hand', or to give an example referring to the past, 'Until the early nineteenth century steam engines could pump water to a height of no more than 30 feet.' The reason why this restriction applied to all steam engines of the period is that no boilers capable of generating the necessary high pressure steam were produced until Trevithick did so in 1800. The explanatory force of the 'quasi-law' about steam pumps is derived entirely from such physical facts as that steam generated at the ordinary boiling point of 100°C has a pressure equal to the atmosphere, a pressure equal to that of a 30-foot column of water. There is nothing to be gained by grouping together technological truths and rule-derived practices as being loosely law-like statements. The two types have different backing and, more important, are not laws of either a loosely or lightly knit kind.

It is true, of course, that the distinction between exceptionless generalizations and generalizations which hold only as a rule—which are loosely law-like—is an important one. A sociologist often speaks of a people's tendency to follow a custom or to exhibit a certain kind of regularity of behaviour or to be guided knowingly by a particular social rule. In doing so he implies that the people sometimes act otherwise, that even in appropriate conditions they commonly, but not always, react in these ways. The people in question tend, though only tend, to act in a regular fashion or to conform to certain standards. Some of Blalock's propositions can be rephrased, without change of meaning, as tendency statements. Thus the assertion that given open resources, 'slavery or serfdom is unlikely if there is no widespread need for cheap, unskilled labor',[1] can be rewritten as 'slavery or serfdom tend to be absent if . . .' Because of this possibility, social regularities, which may be either exceptionless or tendencies, can be confused on the one hand with universal causal laws, and on the other hand with statistical laws. This confusion is made easier by the ambiguous use of 'tendency'. For example, in saying that slavery tends to be absent 'if there is no need for cheap, unskilled labor' we may be making any one of three distinct claims: (1) that

[1] Blalock, *op. cit.*, p. 51.

usually, but not always, no slaves are present; (2) that only a few slaves, at most, are ever present; (3) that usually, but not always, only a few slaves are present. All three claims can be phrased as tendency statements; they do not profess to give sufficient conditions for either the complete absence of all slaves under this condition (a universal law), or the absence of some proportion of them (a statistical law). We commonly employ tendency statements when we cannot supply empirical generalizations which tell us how often the tendencies will hold, or which describe with any exactitude the properties in question. Because of this employment, it is fatally easy to think of rule-exemplifying behaviour *not* as guided by a tendency to follow certain rules, but as governed by a certain behavioural tendency—by a loosely law-like generalization that may eventually be converted into a statistical or universal law of social behaviour.

Chapter six

1. Social law or social regularity?

Now there is no doubt that sociologists often find it difficult to distinguish, with the evidence at their disposal in actual situations, between the exemplification of social rules, regularities, and practices on the one hand, and genuine social laws on the other. How does this problem arise in specific cases? Consider these three propositions which will serve to illustrate the difficulty of drawing the distinction in some particular instances. (1) 'The greater the importance of high individual performance to the productivity of the work group, the lower the degree of minority discrimination by employers.' (2) 'The greater the competition among employers for persons with high performance levels, the lower the degree of minority discrimination by employers.' (3) 'The easier it is accurately to evaluate an individual's performance level, the lower the degree of minority discrimination by employers.' In each case it is assumed that the prestige level of the work and conditions of the labour market remain constant.[1]

These propositions assert that discrimination against a minority group by employers will vary inversely with: 'the importance of high individual performance to productivity', competition for able employees, and ease of evaluating an employee's performance. The truth of these assertions obviously depends upon the truth of some additional unstated assumptions. Chief among these is that employers seek to maximize profits in a rational way. This claim, at first sight, is a weak tendency statement with the usual *ceteris paribus* clause; a counter-example would be a competitive employer who did not seek to maximize profits. There are, of course, such employers. Another, though less general, assumption is that employers value high productivity enough to choose it rather than the lower produc-

[1] These examples are taken from Blalock, *op. cit.*, 98.

tivity resulting from discrimination. A third assumption is that the individual worker's performance is not restricted by group conventions about levels of output. A fourth is that discrimination is not so severe that members of the minority group are *never* eligible for the employment pool. More might be listed, but this fact in itself is unimportant. Every well-formed hypothesis in the natural sciences is similarly dependent on an accompanying gloss.[1] The crucial point here is whether after all these assumptions have been stated—or supplied on demand—the hypothesis, as given, passes relevant tests of its truth. In the present case, the last two assumptions of the four just mentioned are supplied to us as consequences of related hypotheses; and no doubt some additional, and more specific, qualifications of the scope of the hypothesis, or of the limits of the conditions under which it is asserted to apply, could be given when needed.

The process of providing qualifications of this kind is a necessary requirement for settling the question whether the hypothesis so qualified asserts a social law or a mere social regularity. For until we have decided that the hypothesis holds of all, or of some fixed proportion of cases, past, present, and future, under the circumstances provided by the gloss, we shall be in doubt as to whether the conjunction of properties is law-like or not—whether we have mistaken merely rule-guided behaviour for law-like activity. However, the problem raised by our present three examples, and by many other hypotheses in sociology, is that once all the relevant conditions are specified, the assertion becomes either tautologous or false. If we qualify the hypothesis so that it applies to all cases of a certain kind—that is, states a regularity which is unrestricted temporally or spatially—rather than one which simply applies to those of certain places and periods, the hypothesis becomes empirically empty. It no longer has even the appearance of a testable claim about the invariable relationships holding between instances of two or more properties. The qualifications seem to alter the sense of the claim and not merely the field to which it is supposed to refer.

For example, there are societies in which employers are always members of their own work groups. These employers compete vigorously against each other for able employees, but it occasionally happens that an employer refuses to hire anyone he thinks to be more able than himself. Now if in such a society most of the available working members of a particular minority were thought, by such an employer, to be more able than himself, he might well discriminate against them in his hiring policy. In that case our second proposition, which asserted that minority discrimination varies inversely with the

---

[1] See my *Explanation in Social Science*, London and Chicago, 1963, pp. 147–56.

competition for able employees, would not be true. Of course, the proposition could be altered to read 'The greater the competition among employers for *any* persons with high performance levels, the lower the degree of minority discrimination by employers'. However, this alteration would have the obvious disadvantage of making the proposition a tautology. For if the employers competed to hire *any* able person with the relevant abilities, then it would follow logically that they would compete for any able minority member with those abilities, and discrimination would necessarily be bound to decrease correspondingly.

Hence our counter-example shows that the proposition *as stated* is not an assertion of a universal law. The proposition simply characterizes a social regularity which is limited to particular, specifiable times and places. It is a regularity that is based on peculiar and easily changeable circumstances which are not taken account of in its assertion. Because these circumstances are unrecognized until revealed by a counter-example, either actual or imagined, the hypotheses which they support do not contain any explicit reference to them. For instance, we should immediately recognize as an assertion of social regularity the remark, 'In Malaysia since Independence, discrimination against the Chinese by employers has varied inversely with the competition for able employees.' But only some form of testing by counter-example will tell us that the statement, 'Discrimination against minority employees varies inversely with competition for able employees', describes neither the necessary nor sufficient conditions for lowering the degree of minority discrimination by employers *per se*.

To this criticism of the truth of our original hypothesis, the obvious response is to try to restrict the class of employers in a manner which will make the statement true. We then can test the revised statement by means of counter-examples, actual or imagined, in the same way as we did the previous one. If the new statement fails this test, we have three options. We can try, once again, to recast its scope: that is, to redescribe the properties or classes of objects to which the statement applies. We can alter our description of the causal connection between the properties. Or we can abandon the statement as irremediably false. To choose any of these alternatives is to admit that the statement as given fails to supply us with a law.

On the other hand, what if the revised statement passes this test? And then passes further tests of this kind? Do we still have to find out by additional testing, either direct or indirect, whether the supposed inverse correlation between competition for able employees and discrimination by employers actually holds within the limits set? Clearly not; for the test of our ability to restrict the class of employers in a suitable way is the same test as that of discovering whether the inverse correlation holds with respect to this new class. It is logically impossible for us to perform the first without also performing the second.

2. Can social laws have policy-dependent terms?

Now nothing about such a *test procedure* distinguishes this sort of case from successful cases found in natural science, cases in which we can describe a hypothesis and its accompanying gloss without uttering either a tautology or a falsehood. What other difference between the two fields, then, results in the candidates from the natural sciences being so much more successful than the candidates from the social sciences? The difference obviously lies in the kinds of questions pursued in the two fields, and hence, in the kinds of evidence used in answering them. Sociologists commonly find themselves discovering social regularities rather than social laws because so many of their problems and procedures ensure that result. Until those are changed, the oscillation between falsity and triviality in the case of law claims will continue unchecked.

Let us see how this result is brought about by the character of the topics that sociologists 'choose' to discuss. For this purpose we can use, once again, the example of discrimination against minority groups, for it incorporates all the necessary elements. A minority group, according to the definition we discussed earlier, is self-segregated, is the object of prejudice, and is discriminated against by a dominant group. Now a prejudice, we said, is a refusal to be guided by rational argument; discrimination the putting into practice of judgments about people that are not based solely on their appropriate individual qualifications. Segregation, self-imposed or not, is the geographical separation which is produced by discrimination.

We concluded that because it is impossible to give a *general* characterization of individual qualifications, it is not possible to give a sociologically useful definition of all forms of discriminatory treatment. What is to count as discrimination of a certain kind is determined by social policy, by the public standard adopted for that sort of situation. Obviously, these standards will, and do, vary from one society to another, differ within different sections of the same society, and change with time. Such judgments of social policy are made, and take effect, in particular societies at specific times and places. Hence, the definition of 'minority group'—into which segregation, prejudice, and discrimination enter as defining properties —will incorporate the notion of appropriate public standards concerning prejudice and discrimination. The effect of this will be to make impossible the recognition, or picking out, of any particular minority group without our employing some judgment of social

107

policy about what specific activities are prejudicial and discriminatory. The mere definition of 'minority group' will not by itself provide us with a means of recognizing a minority group, since what is to count as such a group will depend entirely upon which particular social standard is adopted for characterizing any given sort of behaviour as discriminatory treatment or due to prejudice.

We can now indicate how this fact about the definition of 'minority group' bears upon the prospects for success of our three propositions concerning discrimination by employers. These propositions assert that such discrimination against a minority group varies inversely with the employee's performance, testability of his performance, and his scarcity value. We assume that each of these latter three properties can be appropriately defined and measured in such a way that it will be applicable to any society, past, present or future. The question remaining, then, is how we can characterize *in general*, and thus measure, 'the degree of minority discrimination by employers'. For we have been saying that the cases which fall under this heading are placed there by our use of particular, and competing, judgments of social policy. A case of discrimination under one policy may not be such a case under another policy. For example, not everyone accepts, or need accept, the view that differential employment of women workers is discriminatory treatment of a minority group.

Thus there are six possible answers to our query about the prospects of success. The answers are: (a) that we can provide a general characterization of the terms 'employer' and 'minority discrimination', and can reasonably look for social laws which utilize them; (b) that we can provide more specific characterizations—those of certain kinds of employers and certain kinds of discrimination—which our law assertions will have to employ; (c) that we can provide both sorts of characterizations and both sorts of law assertions; (d) that we can provide neither characterizations nor laws; (e) that we can provide the specific characterizations but no corresponding law; (f) that we can provide general characterizations but no corresponding laws. Let us begin with (a).

We may well be able to give a general characterization of the term 'employer', but can we do this for the phrase 'minority discrimination by employer'? According to the arguments advanced in chapter two, the only useful general characterization will read, 'differential treatment not based on a difference of individual qualifications alone, but based at least in part on other factors'. Since the distinction between individual qualifications and other factors is drawn as a consequence of the social policy adopted, the individual qualifications being referred to on any given occasion will vary accordingly; and so, of course, will the other factors, such as race, religion, or ethnic origin. As we saw, on some policies a particular religious faith is taken to be an individual qualification for certain jobs, whereas on other policies any such religious requirement is classified as discriminatory. Our general propositions about discrimination, therefore, will have to replace the phrase 'minority discrimination by employer' with the clause 'differential treatment not based on a difference of individual qualifications alone'.

When we make the appropriate substitution in our second proposition it becomes: 'The greater the competition among employers for persons with high performance levels, the lower the degree of differential treatment that is not based on a difference of individual qualifications alone.' Taken at face value, this proposition is a tautology. It merely asserts that the readier an employer is to hire able people, the less ready he is to ignore them because of certain of their other qualities: that is, those qualities not relevant to their ability. The qualities are not specified, and their type is indicated only by contrast with high performance. But can the proposition be reworded so as to become an empirical one? Clearly not, unless we can specify some of the other qualities. For if we do not do this, we have no way of distinguishing them from the relevant qualifications. Our proposition continues to make the empty claim that the more interested the employer is in hiring able people, the more likely he will be to ignore those of their qualities which he thinks of as irrelevant to their performance. We might reword the proposition, then, by mentioning at least one quality other than high performance. For instance, we might try this: 'The greater the competition among employers for persons with high performance levels, the lower the degree of reliance placed on the applicants' racial membership.' The objection to this proposition, once again, is that there are situations, easily described, of which it will not be true. If the employers in a particular society are firmly wedded to the principle of probable indicators, the fact that an applicant belongs to a certain race will be taken as an accurate sign of his lack of ability. In order for the proposition to hold, then, the employers have to be willing to test performance independently of racial membership. That is, they must agree that racial membership is sometimes not a relevant qualification. Yet when we grant this point, we then are confronted with the sort of counter-example produced earlier against this proposition: that employers might refuse to hire anyone they thought more able than themselves. To exclude this, and many other possible counter-examples, we must make the proposition tautological. For the mere mention of some quality other than high performance will not help. The quality mentioned has to be taken by the employers as being independent of high performance, as being, in short, an irrelevant property of the applicant; and by taking account of this we turn our proposed law statement into a tautology once more. Since this objection applies to any property that we care to take—for example, sex, religion, ethnic origin—all three of our proposed laws fall to the same blow.

Of the six possible answers that we listed, only the negative one (d) is true: that we can provide neither the appropriate characterizations nor the relevant laws when policy-terms are essential to both. It does not matter whether the characterizations are more general or less general; we have seen that the same difficulties arise equally in the case of 'minority discrimination by employers' and 'racial discrimination by employers'. The difficulties lie in our inability to give unique sets of properties for determining such classes as recognizable minority discriminators or recognizable racial discriminators. We can define the class 'minority discriminator' or the class 'racial discriminators' but not in such a way as to allow us to recognize the members by means of the definition alone. We require the additional information which comes from a policy judgment as to what counts as a minority group and as discrimination against it. Because this information is, or could be, supplied by different policies, it cannot be incorporated into a single definition which describes a unique set of properties. Yet without such a set we cannot uniquely determine a corresponding class of (recognizable) members. And if we cannot do that, then we certainly cannot produce any law-like statements which assert invariable associations between classes or *recognizable* members.

The same conclusions hold of all those terms whose adoption depends, in the way indicated, on judgments of value or policy. At the end of chapter two some of these terms were mentioned: among them were 'delinquent', 'social deviant', 'alienation', 'undue deference', 'successful rehabilitation', and 'criminal behaviour'. These terms, it was said, 'embody the notion of observable divergence from an appropriate public standard for the kind of behaviour in question'. Since these standards are rules which can and do vary from place to place and from one time to another, the definitions of these terms do not uniquely determine classes of recognizable members. Therefore, we cannot use these terms to construct plausible statements of law-like connections between classes (or properties).

But, of course, terms which refer to deviations from public standards are only a part of the set of sociological terms whose adoption is similarly a matter of policy judgment. There are also terms which refer to the successful achievement of various public standards. Examples of such terms are: 'successful rehabilitation', 'due deference', 'socially assimilated', 'equitable distribution of services and income', 'high social status', 'adequate pension', 'fair wage', 'residential integration', 'free speech', 'social solidarity', and 'non-discriminatory treatment'. The list can be extended indefinitely. What is to count as an example of due deference or social assimilation or an adequate pension will depend on the standards adopted in each sort of case. Which standards are adopted is a matter of value judgment that may vary widely within each society and from one society to another. Hence, here no more than in connection with terms of divergence from standards can we supply laws which correlate the 'properties' to which such terms are applicable. For instance, we cannot argue that whatever our criteria of free speech, it is found only in societies with high social solidarity—whatever our criteria of that may be.

It will do no good to reply, 'But if we are not entitled to assert a universal statement that makes this sort of use of policy-dependent terms, what entitles us to assert a non-universal statement which makes it?' The answer is simple. A statement of social regularity does not raise the problem of divergent judgments of social policy. By restricting its claim to particular times and places, the statement gives us information which allows us to determine what counts, for that group of people, as an instance of the relevant property. Take the example used earlier: 'In Malaysia since 1965, discrimination against the Chinese by employers has varied inversely with the competition for able employees.' Here we know when and where to look for instances of the supposed inverse correlation. For Malaysians of the period indicated, the Chinese are the chief minority group. The claim that employment discrimination against them has varied inversely with competition is false, since it has been government policy to strengthen the economic position of the Malayans as against that of the Chinese by ensuring that Malayan applicants are hired. In contrast, the law-like statement, 'In every society of a certain kind, discrimination against the chief minority group by employers varies inversely with competition for all employees', gives us no such information about a genuine class of chief minority groups or what is to count as discrimination against them. These groups are selected differently by different policies, and so discrimination is differently selected. Because the groups do not make up the membership of one empirically useful class, the groups cannot have, and so cannot be discovered to have, the law-like relationships which one such class can display with another. In short, a statement of social regularity, like that about Malaysia, succeeds because it attributes properties merely to a collection of items rather than to a class defined by a common property. But an assertion of law must fail when it attributes properties merely to a collection and not to such a class.

The terms which we have been examining are not the names of empirically useful classes. Since they are not, it is natural to suggest that they might be if the sociologist were to determine the policies

111

under which they are applied. The suggestion is that the sociologist could produce his own policy-free definitions of 'minority group' or 'criminal behaviour' or 'undue deference' or 'fair wage'. He might then be able to use these definitions to produce empirical generalizations about the members of the genuine classes to which the definitions applied. The standards adopted might not be public but they would be uniform. Surely there would be no insuperable problem in giving such definitions of all the policy-dependent terms?

But it is not true that the supplying of such definitions by the sociologist presents no insuperable problem. On the contrary, it is clear that their attempted provision would not produce the desired results. The sociologist, like anyone else, has to choose his policies, and once he has chosen them, their consequences are the same as if anyone else had selected them. Thus if our previous conclusions about minority discrimination were correct, the only useful *general* definition of it will be, 'differential treatment not based on a difference of individual qualifications alone'. Which these are will vary with the policy adopted, and it, in turn, will decide the behaviour that is to be classified as discriminatory. For the sociologist to adopt a view as to what will be instances of discriminatory behaviour in each and every society, past, present, and future, is perfectly legitimate. In fact, it is inescapable if he wishes to study what *he* takes to be discriminatory treatment, no matter where and when it occurs, and to formulate law-like generalizations about this treatment. What he must not do, however, is to believe that his way of picking out cases of discrimination or free speech or anomie is determined by their possession of a common natural property, like shape, weight, colour, taste or flammability, which he recognizes independently of his policy judgment and about which he can formulate laws. The property which his cases all share is that of falling under his rule of selection. That they are picked out by his standard, if they are, is a fact about its employment and not about some common property which they possess independently of that standard. The use of the standard creates, rather than presupposing, that property in common.

Now it is obviously important to understand exactly what is revealed by the policy-dependence of these sociological terms. Earlier in this chapter it was asserted that sociologists have not always distinguished two quite different projects: (a) the misguided attempt to identify social laws with descriptions of the various activities of rule-following, making, and breaking displayed in the social behaviour of human beings, and (b) the legitimate attempt to discover social laws underlying this rule-oriented behaviour. The first project confuses the social laws which might account for the rule-oriented behaviour of the members of human groups with the descriptions of the social regularities whose presence is to be explained. The second project does not make this mistake. When a sociologist uses policy-dependent terms like 'discrimination', 'prejudice', and 'criminal' in statements of law, and does not give those terms an explicit operational specification, when, that is, he uses those non-operational terms and asserts universally constant associations between the supposed classes to which the terms are thought to apply, he is making it easy for himself to fall into the former error. For he is taking a statement such as 'In every society of a certain specifiable kind, employment discrimination against a minority group will vary inversely with the ease of evaluating an employee's performance' to be a social law. And he takes it to be a social law because he has used a policy-dependent term like 'discrimination' to help to generate a law-like assertion from another, more specific claim about particular times and places. For that more specific claim he is able to give his policy-dependent term an operational specification, e.g. 'In the private-business sector of the American economy in the mid-twentieth century, employment discrimination (specified as follows) will vary inversely with the ease of evaluating an employee's performance.' When the sociologist drops the spatio-temporal indicators from this statement of an American social regularity, and also drops, unwittingly, the operational specification of 'discrimination', he is left with what he mistakenly thinks is a straightforward generalization of his original claim. It is a generalization of that claim, but not a straightforward one. The sociologist has left *implicit* in the new, law-like assertion the various special conditions of time, place, social rules of race relations, economic development, and so forth, which were given more explicitly in the earlier statement. That they are implicit can be seen by the sociologist's reliance upon them when counter-examples are urged against his new, law-like assertion. It then becomes clear that he has been *assuming*, first, that the local rules and rule-oriented behaviour on which his original statement was based evidentially, and, second, that a particular interpretation of discrimination, hold everywhere within the scope of his generalization. He is then treating certain local rules, or rather the social regularities of behaviour which result, for example, from rule-following, as instantiations of the laws of society. The use of non-operational policy-dependent terms encourages this mistake because they seem to offer a way of generalizing from statements about, e.g. changes in employment discrimination in New York, 1950–60, to changes in employment discrimination everywhere at any time, or to changes in some class of places during certain sorts of periods. Since there can be no laws of discrimination, or criminality, or prejudice when these terms are not operationally specified, local social regularities cannot be the instantiations of such laws. But

113

to say that the activities of people in a group are rule-*guided* is obviously different from saying that those same activities are law-*governed*. In particular, the legitimate attempt to describe the behaviour regularities which result from rule-following, making, and breaking in a given society, or in a collection of societies, or even in a class of societies, does not *in itself* justify any attempt to describe those regularities as being either the instantiation of, or the result of, the operation of social laws. Thus describing the local rules or classes of local rules which make essential use of policy-dependent terms, specifically interpreted, is one step; stating laws which explain the presence or development or inter-relations of classes of such local rules is another and quite distinct step.

3. Additional problems in distinguishing laws from regularities

There is another reason why it is sometimes difficult to distinguish between a social regularity and a social law. Suppose, for example, we discover that each employee of the lens-fitting room of a certain factory deliberately follows the practice of setting his output at a level not very far above that of the slowest worker in the group. Suppose, also, that we discover the same unofficial convention in many other groups that work to piece-rates under a factory system. We then have the problem of how best to describe the occurrence of this regularity. We may think that the convention of stabilizing the output is simply the result of an attempt to realize a common goal, namely that of protection of the weakest member. But is the striving for this goal under certain conditions—those of the lens-fitters, for instance—a mere social regularity? Or is this activity to be described differently, as an example of a rather narrow but genuine social law which can be subsumed under more general social laws?

Which answer we give will depend on how we account for the employees' *apparent* effort to protect their weakest member—what we take their goal to be. If we think that it is a disinterested activity to which they have been trained, the attempt may be classified as mere conformity to a social convention, that of stabilizing the output, in order to achieve the group's conventional goal of protecting its weakest member. On the other hand, if we believe that the employees are actually trying to prevent the piece-rate from being lowered, and that protection of the slow worker is simply a side effect of the means they have chosen, then we may think that stabilizing the output is an instance of psychological law: that no man, if he can prevent it, will work harder for a reward which he earlier obtained more easily. This interpretation rejects the view that output stabilization is the direct result of trying to protect the group's weakest member. Instead, the stabilization policy is taken to have a different goal and a different kind of explanation: that is, one in terms of law instantiation rather than mere rule conformity.

In actual situations the three factors which encourage confusion between descriptions of regularities and laws, namely, lack of testing, the use of policy-dependent terms, and disagreement about classification, often interact. Sometimes the very question at issue is whether a particular social rule, norm, convention, or standard is operating. This question arises because it is not clear how the activity being studied is best to be described and classified. Are those people milling about in order to show their political sympathies, to welcome a visitor, to organize a strike, or to prepare for tomorrow's ceremony? Or are they merely looking for the buses which were promised? We may not be able to decide on the evidence available to us. But which tests we think are required may well depend, in part, on which social policies we have adopted. 'Striking only for an adequate pension' is one description and 'Trying only to intimidate employers' is another, and competitive, description. Employing the latter rather than the former may be the result of believing that pensions are already more than adequate, and that the workers know this. A person who thinks so will look for further evidence of a different kind, and apply different tests, from a person who thinks that bettering their pension is the workers' only goal.

In addition to the factors which made it difficult to distinguish laws from regularities in specific cases, there is a more general factor that encourages the conflation of social laws and social rules. This is the tendency of sociologists, like other scientists, constantly to widen the scope of their generalizations. When sociologists account for a piece of behaviour by showing that it is rule-guided, or rule-breaking, or rule-establishing, they do not usually rest content with that. They must cope with a long series of questions which immediately arise: 'Why does this piece of behaviour conform to these rules while that piece of behaviour does not? Under what social conditions are various kinds of group-standards likely to spread to other groups, or to be resisted by them? In what circumstances do particular types of social conventions arise or decline? How do different sorts of rules, conventions, norms, and standards interact? Why do different rules, and different sorts of rules, diffuse within the same group at such varying rates? In any case of competitive conventions within a group, what kinds of factors permit some to co-exist, some to win out, and others to disappear?' Questions such as these obviously cannot be answered in terms of the rules to which people conform. For the chief point of the questions is to discover why certain sorts of rules are present in a group or why certain sorts of rules are absent. The reply, if a useful one can be given, must be in terms of causal conditions and not in terms of successful rule-following or rule-violation. But the attempt to give such a reply is peculiarly exposed to the hazards of testing, classification, and policy-dependence which we have been discussing. In asserting as a law, for example, that discrimination by employers varies inversely with the ease of evaluating an employee's performance, we are assuming that the quality of this performance is of great consequence to any employer whatsoever. We are assuming, in fact, a wider law to the effect that increased work productivity will count for more with the employer than will any other consequence of his hiring policy. That the assumption is false—that it holds only within certain societies at certain times and hence is at best a social regularity which those societies exhibit—might be shown by testing and evidence. Thus the failure of this wider law-claim would represent a failure to explain, with its aid, why in specific societies the local discrimination against employees varies inversely with the ease of evaluating their individual performance.

Examples of this kind illustrate the special difficulty which appears when we try to explain rule-following in terms of causal laws: that is, when we try to widen the scope of our generalizations. Because of the problem created by policy-dependent terms, and by our testing and classification procedures, we are prone to substitute social regularities for social laws without realizing that we are doing so. The result of this substitution, as we have tried to show, is a constant fluctuation between a claim so heavily qualified that it becomes a tautology and a social regularity so obviously false that it never becomes a plausible law-candidate.

4. Sociological topics and rule-oriented behaviour

We must now look more closely at the connection between this tendency to substitute statements of regularities for statements of laws and the tendency of sociologists to concentrate on certain kinds of topics and problems. For while we wish to show that the former is a consequence of the latter, we have not, so far, characterized those topics and problems in any helpful way. We have pointed out that the use of policy-dependent terms is one cause, at least, of the substitution tendency; but the relationship of these terms to the problems in question has yet to be considered. Nor have we discussed the more general relation between certain topics of sociological concentration and the unwanted scarcity of plausible law-claims. It will be convenient to begin with the broader problem; the use of policy-dependent terms falls under it as a special case.

Sociologists often characterize their field as the study of social order and disorder, as the study of the fundamental regularities which are exhibited in the social behaviour of human beings. These regularities, as we have seen, are of very different kinds. There are the apparent regularities displayed by the formation of simpler social relationships into complex systems: couples form families, and they form communities which unite into political units. There are also the regularities that seem to be expressed in, or by, basic social processes like integration, deviance, control, conflict, indoctrination, co-operation, and stratification. Finally, there are the regularities thought to be associated with the functioning of institutions, institutions of which the family, the company, the sect, the political party, the recreational club, are typical examples. Within any human society, or sub-system of that society, all three kinds of regularities are taken to be present. The sociologist's basic task, therefore, seems to amount to this: he must describe, explain, and predict the change, or absence of change, between any two states of a given social system or any given set of such systems. The chief problem, apparently, is to discover why this task should have proven to be so difficult.

Earlier we suggested that the solution would lie in recognizing that many of the sociologist's questions and procedures ensured the discovery of social regularities rather than social laws. But what is the basis of that prediction? Its basis lies in the fact that much, though by no means all, of the subject matter of sociology consists in the rule-oriented behaviour of people. Their institutions, and many of the social processes which those institutions incorporate, represent complexes of rule-following activity. Business corporations, government departments, universities, assembly lines in factories, missionary sects, dog pounds, and city councils have that much in common. The activity of each requires that its staff perform specified duties in specified ways at particular times. Their duties may or may not be performed by standard operating procedures, governed by a bureaucratic chain of command, sub-divided into departments with distinct functions. It is sufficient if the work is carried out by a voluntary association, for even its members will follow certain rules, whether these be regulations, laws, by-laws, departmental procedures, job conventions, or rules of thumb practised in common.

Similarly, every member of any social organization has at least one role to perform in it; and a member's role is a set of rules which describe both his legitimate tasks and the socially supported claims by other people for the services rendered by him in the performance of those tasks. Being the eldest son in a patriarchal family, a grazier, a member of the local bowling club, an Air Force reserve officer, and secretary of the district Conservation Society, are roles of varying scope which one man can play. In doing so he takes account,

117

more or less, of the rights and obligations in which each role consists. That is, his behaviour conforms or fails to conform to certain standards and conventions; it is more or less appropriate. When his behaviour conforms, he is obviously rule-guided. When his behaviour fails to conform to particular standards, it may still be rule-guided, for non-conformity in one role is sometimes the result of conformity in another role: a poor husband was often a gallant lover.

Now since customs, or standardized ways of behaving, cluster into roles, and roles into institutions, and these, in turn, combine into systems, a great deal of the sociologist's attention must be fixed on rule-following, rule-violating, and rule-making activity. Much of his effort, then, will be directed toward obtaining information about the social regularities which such activity produces. He may be interested, for example, in whether a given society possesses formal hierarchies of deference and whether these conflict with the informal patterns of deference in subsidiary organizations. Or he may try to discover how initiative and innovation are systematically discouraged in a particular bureaucracy; or to what skills a society gives its highest financial rewards; or how various societies differ in the extent to which they provide formal indicators of the social distance between people, and whether this is done by accent, modes of address, costume, or by some other means.

An interest in such regularities is certainly not an interest in social laws, even when the existence of the regularity is used to explain the presence of a specific piece of behaviour. In learning that a particular Hopi will not sell his land because the Hopi people do not treat their land as a private commodity, the sociologist has been referred to a custom of that society and not to a law of a certain kind of society. It is true that the Hopi practice is not confined to them. But that several, or even all, societies have a particular custom hardly shows it to be a law of those societies. Nor need the universal presence of a custom or of a social regularity always require explanation in terms of laws. An explanation may be given by means of what is thought to be a more general social practice which subsumes the explicandum. Thus the universal presence of incest taboos of some kind often has been explained as a special case of the widespread social practice of eliminating conflict of role within the residential family, of consolidating the nuclear group. The rights and obligations of a husband and son would easily clash if the same person took both parts. But it has also been argued that the practice is really a social law. Whether it is law or mere regularity, the avoidance of role conflict might be accounted for, in turn, as a means of preserving amicable relationships between the bride's relatives and those of the groom, relationships which, in the circumstances, are necessary for the proper functioning of the remainder of the social system.

At some point, of course, an explanation in terms of rule-conformity (or rule-violation) will no longer suffice. The question 'Why this sort of universal practice rather than some other sort?' will have to be given an answer that does not merely refer to rule-following, since not *every* rule can be followed because still other rules are followed. The answer may be historical in that it refers to the origins of the practice, to the stages of its development, or to both. The answer may be theoretical in that it explicitly cites empirical generalizations and does not merely presuppose them. Or the answer may describe the effects of the practice on the maintenance of a self-persisting system to which the practice belongs; but since prediction and explanation in terms of functions commit us to asserting laws applicable to the system, a functional answer is merely a special type of the theoretical account. Now which kind of answer is given will depend on how the investigator phrases his question, and thus on what he wants to know. If he is not clear about the latter and hence about the former, he will obtain what he often gets, an indiscriminate mixture of answers.

To be professionally interested in the workings of human societies is to be largely concerned with the regularities of behaviour the societies' members display in pursuing their goals. The force of this trivial truth is inescapable: a very considerable range of the sociologist's questions are directed specifically toward obtaining information about the existence, functioning, relationships, and history of particular complexes of rule-following, rule-violating, and rule-making activities. He wants to know how *this* political party, clan, marriage system, police force, criminal court, or advertising campaign is organized; how it works; who staffs it; what success it has had; what its history in *this* society has been. All these questions, and many others, characteristically yield answers which describe the operation of a set of conventions as exhibited in the behaviour of a particular social group. That is, the answers give us some of the working details of a particular institution, organization, or activity. The answers do not give us more than that, any more than learning similar details about Australian Rules football gives us social (or causal) laws concerning one kind of football. We learn the rules which players of Australian football are expected to follow, as well as the regularities of their rule-following behaviour: the techniques and strategies the players employ, the differences between successful and unsuccessful teams and their players, the illegal behaviour indulged in and guarded against. Having learned all this, we have learned a lot about the regular course of a certain type of Australian rule-following activity. But in learning both the football rules and the regularities of actual play we have not learned causal laws of football or causal laws of athletics, even though from those rules and regularities we may be able to infer, with the aid of certain details about today's match, the name of the winning team.

Against this it cannot correctly be suggested that in going on to ask questions about *types* of social activity the sociologist ought to obtain answers about the laws exemplified by those types. For the types are defined, and thus identified, by means of the kinds of rules or conventions which they exemplify and not by the social laws they may or may not illustrate. A matrilineal clan, for example, consists of people who by various rules trace their origin, through women alone, to the same female ancestor. A feud is a permanent, hostile relationship between two lineage groups, but it is carried on by means of conventions as well recognized as that whose breach began the hostility. The potlatch party, in which large amounts of useful goods were destroyed or given away, was a ceremonial part of a prestige-competition that determined, by rules, social rank in the society. The fact that sociologists are concerned with *types* of social relationship tells us only that they deal with types of rule-complexes, not that the types are formed and operate according to social laws.

The situation is no different in the case of policy-dependent terms. In giving empirical specifications for 'discriminatory employment' or 'delinquent' or 'relative deprivation', we are adopting standards and rules for the classification of cases. In adhering to such standards we are guiding our behaviour by their means; and to do this is simply to engage in one form of rule-guided activity. The sociological study of discriminatory employment or delinquency or relative deprivation will be the study of a certain type of regular behaviour which results from the influence of rules. These topics, and the questions arising from them, do not differ in any relevant way from those we have been discussing under the label 'social regularities'. The reason, then, why 'discrimination' and 'delinquency' do not refer to measurable properties of theoretical interest is the same reason why the terms 'to potlatch' or 'to have an adequate pension' do not. It is that all of them refer to the rule-guided behaviour of a social group and not to instantiations of its law-governed activity. Social laws might be used to account for certain features of that rule-guided behaviour. But doing that would be quite distinct from trying to apply social laws *directly* to something called 'discriminatory' or 'delinquent' behaviour. The regularities, if any, which are discernible in the situation of the juvenile delinquents of Melbourne—their origin in broken homes, their working-class background, their preference for car stealing—obviously need not be those present among the juvenile delinquents of Saigon or Manila. If there are laws of juvenile delinquency, they must *explain* the presence of such regularities and not be identical with them, even when the regularity has so general a form as 'being frustrated by an inability to satisfy one's rising expectations by legal means'. Since only some frustrated youth become known law-breakers while most frustated youth do not, the intended problem here remains obscure. For it is implausible to believe that the question 'Why do some youths become known law-breakers?' is any more sensible than the question why some adults become known law-breakers. The only general answer, in both cases, is that their training in observance of the laws has been no more successful than their avoidance of detection after breaking them. This answer is not the statement of a social law.

5. The task of sociological laws

We began this chapter by asking what impels sociologists constantly 'to bring forward as empirical hypotheses a set of candidates which are either trivially true or obviously false'. We now have an answer. What impels them is the same confusion that is largely responsible, in sociology, for the production of inadequate definitions, pseudo-properties, and ill-phrased problems. The confusion is that between: one, the regularities of behaviour which come from trying to follow, or from failing to follow, the rules and conventions of a social group and, two, the regularities of behaviour described by the law statements which try to account for the origin, presence, and operation of those rules, or for their failure to operate. Examples of the former regularities are: the prevalence of juvenile delinquents from broken homes; the adjustment of individual performance to a level sanctioned by the work group; the favouring by employers of high productivity in their work force; the inverse correlation between minority discrimination and competition for able employees. But what about examples of the latter, examples of law statements which are thought to explain such regularities?

The prevalence of juvenile delinquents from broken homes is often given a psychological explanation; we might offer as a candidate the statement 'Children who feel unloved by their parents will refuse to show goodwill toward other people by obeying their laws.' This is false as it stands, but at least broken homes are classified by it as merely one type of loveless background, and that background has some plausibility as a causal factor in the production of delinquency. Again, the adjustment of individual performance to a level sanctioned by the work group might be explained as a case of the agent wishing to preserve group approval. The relevant law-claim might be put as, 'People who wish to obtain the rewards of participation in a cohesive work group must be able to agree on the work goals and work standards which that group will pursue.' This claim assumes, of course, that 'cohesive work group' can be defined independently of 'pursuit of work goals and standards'. If this cannot be done, the claim will be trivially true and thus useless. The favouring by employers of high productivity in their work force can be explained in terms of the employers' goal of maximizing profits, company growth, company stability, and personal rewards, in the long run. Employers with both this goal and the belief that high productivity is necessary for achieving it will favour such productivity. A similar law claim can be given to explain the inverse correlation between minority discrimination and competition for able employees. If employers believe that their company goals, and hence their personal rewards, require able employees, the employers will try to hire, in conditions of short supply, any able person as long as the side effects of doing so are thought to be compatible with the achievement of the company's goals.

None of these law-candidates is highly plausible, but then none of them has to be. The candidates are produced only to illustrate the difference between the regularities of rule-guided behaviour—for example, work restriction, high productivity, lowered discrimination —and the regularities of law-governed behaviour, as in the pursuit of life-sustaining profit, love, and the admiration given by other people. The latter regularities are used to explain the presence of the former in terms of the goals to which the rule-guided behaviour is taken to be the means. But the mere presence of such rule-guided behaviour does not itself explain the pursuit of these goals except when that behaviour is performed only for its own sake.

It is obvious that the explanation of rule-violating behaviour, as in the case of juvenile delinquents from broken homes, must take a different form. The explanation must consist in showing why the rules have not been observed by the agent: for example, why different means have been employed for the same goals or why different goals have been substituted. Feeling unloved by parents is given as a condition sufficient, in the circumstances, for law-breaking by children; they are said either to lack a goal which many people have, that of showing good will toward other people by obeying the law, or to lack the expression of the appropriate attitudes.

In general, then, rule or convention violations set us a different problem from that of rule and convention observance. The problem is that of explaining why the rules, conventions, or taboos have been broken in a particular instance, or set of instances, whereas ordinarily they are not. The answer is that people are trained and taught, usually with considerable success, to observe the conventions of their group. Sometimes, however, this training is unsuccessful, and then the question of interest to the sociologist is 'Why was rule-observance not effective in this case when it is effective elsewhere?' For the most part, the answer will be that some necessary condition for the success of rule-learning has not been met: the crime-ridden street is inhabited by oppressed strangers; the unruly school children know that their careers will be miserable; the young social radicals are the children of parents who were once young radicals. Commonly, the reply will not be in terms of rule-following or its regularities of behaviour. Breaches of rules are only sometimes to be explained as the observance of different rules and the seeking of different ends. However, when breaches *can* be accounted for in this latter way, as in a delinquent's adherence to the conventions of a criminal sub-culture, the regularity of behaviour which is displayed will require the same sort of law-explanation as any other form of rule-observance.

But the interest in this kind of answer does not prevent the sociologist from asking a still different kind of question. The sociologist can also ask why rule-training *is* usually effective, why conventions are so widely followed and so successfully transmitted: why, that is, there has been so much *rule-establishing* behaviour. He can phrase this either as a query about the general conditions of social learning or as a specific question about particular sorts of conventions in particular kinds of situations. In either case, his answer will be in terms of the factors which produce successful rule-learning and successful transmission of that learning. The answer will try to explain the presence of rule-following and will not appeal to it as being the explanation which is required. Hence, if the answer is not to be merely historical, it must refer to social laws rather than to social conventions.

Thus there are at least two types of situations in which rule-following explanations may be irrelevant. One is that of rule-violation. The other is that of explaining the presence, origin, operation, need for, and success of, rules or conventions themselves. But there is a third, and very important, type of situation to which rule-following explanations do not apply. They do not apply to all that socially displayed behaviour which is neither rule-conforming nor rule-violating but is unregulated. Many habitual social practices, or common regularities, are neither prescribed nor proscribed, neither appropriate nor inappropriate: in any particular society, women may frequent cocktail bars in the day-time more than do men; cigars may be favoured by older men, pipes by younger ones; traffic accidents, suicides, and births may decline during the dry season; Irish Catholic immigrants may largely staff the police force. In order to account for these and similar regularities, it will be necessary to refer to such factors as the unanticipated consequences of rule-following or rule violation; to the causal consequences, whether foreseen or not, that conformity to one sort of convention has upon conformity to a conflicting convention; to the effects upon various institutions or customs of new technological, commercial, and industrial practices;

to the results of disasters of various kinds on the structural arrangements of group life. To do any of these is to try to find connections, often causal connections, between the regularities which arise from rule-following or rule-violation and those which arise from some other source.

For this reason, and those given previously in this chapter, it is a *mistake* to think, as many people have, that because so much of sociological inquiry is concerned with describing rule-oriented behaviour, the question 'Do sociological laws exist?' must—logically must—have a negative answer. The answer is open, but the question is not, despite ceremonial protests to the contrary, in the foreground of the sociologist's attention. That foreground is occupied by problems about the regular course of various rule-oriented activities, and in particular, by the way in which specific kinds of group behaviour can be identified, classified, measured, described, and explained in terms of the conventions and norms that such behaviour exemplifies. This is only to be expected. For the questions of immediate sociological, and often practical, interest commonly take the form of a temporal chain: (1) 'What *is* that activity in which those people are engaged?' (2) 'Why are those people performing *that* activity here and now instead of another activity there and then?' (3) 'Under what social conditions do people of that sort engage in that kind of activity at certain times and places?' (4) 'What social laws determine those social conditions?' The first three questions need not, and commonly do not, raise a problem about a social law. They ask whether the activity is rule-guided, what the rules are, and what the social context of their employment is. Only the fourth question asks for a social explanation of that social context. Moreover, in at least some cases that last question will not admit of an answer, for the laws determining the social conditions will be, for example, psychological or physical, and not social.

Critics of the scarcity of sociological laws often forget an elementary but important fact: most sociologists do not devote any large proportion of their working time to a search for sociological laws. The reason for this is twofold. First, most sociologists, most of the time, are not engaged in looking for explanations at all, and so not for explanations in terms of social laws. They identify, classify, measure, report, describe. Second, when sociologists *do* search for explanations, a large proportion of what they are trying to explain does not call for law-explanations, as we have seen, and in particular, does not call for explanations which make essential use of *social* laws. Unfortunately, some sociologists themselves overlook the fact that they and their colleagues are not, for the most part, daily directing themselves to the discovery of social laws. Because they overlook this, it is possible for them to confuse rule-guided with law-governed behaviour, and in consequence to put forward unsuitable candidates for laws, properties, and definitions. But this mistake, as we shall see, does *not* justify the conclusion that sociological generalization is impossible, that the apparent shortage of plausible generalizations is a reliable sign of there being no such things as social laws; and hence of there being no such thing as successful explanation by their means.

Explanations

Chapter seven

1. What should be explained?

When sociology is criticized for its apparent lack of successful explanations, the critic usually concentrates on the apparent absence of explanations which rely on *social* laws. He recognizes that various kinds of other explanations—historical, rule-guided, purposive, for example—are given successfully. He also realizes that many social events and situations are partially explained in terms of physical events and laws. Thus the coastal distribution of the Australian population closely follows the distribution of certain rainfall levels, temperatures, and soils. The consequences of the Black Death in fourteenth-century Europe, of smallpox among the American Indians of the eighteenth century, of fur-trading among the Northeastern Algonkians, of the neglect by the Arabs of the Roman irrigation works in North Africa, are both physical and social. But while the sociologist is interested in the social effect of physical causes, they provide him with no sociological explanations with which to confront his critic. And it is of their absence that the critic complains.

Sociology, as we have seen, is a mixture of different kinds of topics, problems, and answers. If there were no genuine social laws, a great part of sociological investigation would remain unaffected. The chief result would be that law-like explanations would use laws other than sociological ones. The sociologist would simply rely on laws drawn from the other sciences, much as meteorology or political history now do, although the sociologist would not confine himself to an interest in particular events and situations as the historian does. The sociologist's concern with obtaining increasingly general explanations would not be checked. He would still wish to have the answers to the many different sorts of questions which he now asks, but the answers to some of them would be different. The important problem is which of them would be different. However, this problem is merely a variant of the questions, 'What kind of social behaviour can be explained by means of social laws? In what aspect of social life should sociologists be looking for law-governed behaviour— granted that it must be distinguished from rule-governed behaviour in the fashion for which we have been arguing?'

The answers given to these questions in the history of social thought have been exceedingly various. However, all the answers can be classified in terms of two great schisms: that between theories concerning individuals and theories concerning groups; and that between theories concerning rationalistic goal-seeking behaviour and theories concerning behaviour which is not rationalistic, or not goal-directed, or neither rationalistic nor goal-directed. Characteristically, debates about likely areas in which to seek social laws take the form of disagreement on these two basic issues. Should sociologists try to explain the behaviour of individual agents or of groups? Or both? And should that behaviour be chiefly rational choice under conditions of uncertainty and risk, or should other types of behaviour be given pride of place?

Our reply will be determined, in large part, by the importance we give to the different kinds of individual and group activity in social life. Economists who study the calculated and deliberate actions of individual agents tend to think that rational choice is the most important sort of social behaviour to be explained. Social psychologists and some anthropologists tend to think it less important than the non-rational and irrational activity of groups. Social behaviour, they suggest, is best studied when it violates social rules. For then the psychological impulses and dispositions from which social rules protect us stand clearly revealed. It is these impulses and dispositions, after all, which make social regulation a necessity. Ethologists are impressed by the genetic programming of certain types of behaviour, such as language learning and primary social bonding. They are also impressed by the evolutionary background of human social relationships, as well as by the genetic diversity of individual human beings, and hence by their behavioural plasticity rather than by their cultural uniformity. Investigators with preference schedules so different as those of economists, anthropologists, social psychologists, and ethologists are not likely to converge on the same sorts of social behaviour. Nor are these investigators likely to characterize their problems in the same way; and thus they are not likely to look for generalizing explanations of similar situations by similar kinds of laws.

2. The adequacy of rationalistic explanations

Some of the typical questions which arise from such differences of interest and evaluation are illustrated in a discussion on game-theory between J. C. Harsanyi and L. P. Foldes.[1] The former argues that we have to make use of game-theory if we are to explain why people behave as they do in social life. We have to use game-theory, according to Harsanyi, because, first, much of human social behaviour is roughly rational. It represents people's efforts to achieve certain clear-cut goals by using means that have some reasonable chance of producing success. Second, game theory will tell us, as common sense by itself will not, 'how a rational individual would behave in social situations involving cooperation or conflict between two or more individuals.'[2] For this purpose we need to know the goals which people actually pursue, and what they take their own situations to be.

As an example of one goal which is pursued in fact by most people in most societies, Harsanyi uses the case of social status. He advances a theory which he thinks will explain both why some people are given higher status than are others and why anyone ever wants to have a higher status. The theory is that social status is a reciprocal power relationship: the agent who performs services valued by other people in the social group is rewarded by receiving valued services from them. These latter services include deference and esteem. The agent will have high social status to the degree that other people are more dependent on his services than he is on theirs. The initiative in granting high status is taken by those people who have personal reasons for valuing the agent's services. Other people are persuaded by them to support their evaluation of him. The agent's social status is the outcome of tacit bargaining between him and other people concerning the exchange of services.[3] This theory illustrates, its author says, the advantages of rationalistic explanations over those of other kinds, and in particular those which assume 'that social institutions and various forms of social behaviour can be explained in terms of their *social functions*, that is, in terms of the contributions they make to the survival of the society and to the maintenance of its existing institutional framework'.[4] For if the social function of higher social status is to provide an incentive for certain people to accept the burden of important social tasks, why should other people be willing to provide this incentive? Only because they wish to have the task performed, and this is what the rationalistic theory includes as part of its account.

---

[1] Harsanyi, 'Individualistic and Functionalistic Explanations in the Light of Game Theory: The Example of Social Status', and Foldes, 'A Note on Individualistic Explanations'. Both are in *Problems in the Philosophy of Science*, vol. 3, ed. I. Lakatos and A. Musgrave, Amsterdam, 1968, pp. 305–48.

[2] *Op. cit.*, p. 321. [3] *Ibid.*, pp. 317–19. [4] *Ibid.*, p. 305.

Foldes argues, first, that Harsanyi has claimed too much for the useful scope of 'the rationalistic explanation of individual behaviour'. Thus he thinks that we cannot always explain the activities of social organizations like nations and firms as the desired result of the actions of their individual officers. These organizations, Foldes says, often display behaviour as stable, rational, and predictable as that of their staff members. The organizations need to be treated as complete units in themselves, units which interact with other such units and which try to achieve certain goals by rational means. Again, wherever individual behaviour is rigidly and successfully rule-guided or convention-bound, nothing is gained by trying to make use of an explanation in terms of individual goal-seeking by rational agents. For since no effective choice by individual agents is being exercised, their behaviour cannot be explained as the outcome of individual preference. Moreover, there are many social regularities, such as Pareto's law of income distribution, which have no obvious connection with the rational preferences of individual agents. Some of these regularities may be the result of conditioned behaviour, or systematic miscalculation, or unforeseen consequences, or chance processes (the law-like ordering of the outcomes of a series of trials). None of these regularities lends itself to rationalistic explanation.

Foldes goes on to argue that while social norms or conventions are required in explaining the social behaviour of individual agents, the presence and continued existence of these conventions themselves cannot be explained without reference to other social norms. Harsanyi seems to believe that *all* conventions can have their presence explained in terms of the rationally pursued goals of individual people. This, thinks Foldes, is one of the mistakes which Harsanyi's theory of social status exhibits. For much social status is determined by tradition, and this changes so slowly that the status of any given agent may not be explicable as the outcome of tacit bargaining between him and his contemporaries. In cases such as this one, game-theory is not of much explanatory help.

What can we make of this disagreement? There are two basic questions at issue. One is how much social behaviour is eligible, logically, to be explained by rationalistic means, including game theory. The other basic question is whether, given logical eligibility, we are, or will be, able in fact to provide the information about people's actual desires for goals—their motivating forces—which both game theory and rationalistic explanation, in general, require. If we cannot specify what our rational agents are trying to achieve, and cannot determine how much they are prepared to pay for it, we cannot apply the methods which tell us how a fully rational agent would act, given that he had certain information, certain tolerance of risk, and certain goals (or payoff functions). Both questions concern the utility of rationalistic explanations, but the first is directed toward logical requirements and the second toward practical ones.

Now it is clear that much social behaviour is not rationally goal-directed. This is true both of individual people and of organizations or 'corporate persons'. Unintended consequences, both of rational acts and of accidents, are by definition not explicable as the outcome of anything that any person tried to bring about. Yet these consequences demand explanation as much as, if not more than, do the results of calculated acts. If the man I bump against inadvertently on the train station, and thus force on to the track so that he is killed, happens to be the Prime Minister, all sorts of political consequences may follow. The same is true if I bump against him intentionally, not recognizing him but merely disliking his arrogance, and he falls on to the track. What I tried to bring about in this latter case was discomfort to a stranger. What I actually began was a chain of activities that led to a new national election. Part of the explanation of why an election was called at that particular time might be: 'Because the Prime Minister was killed in an accident.' But this is not in itself a rationalistic explanation, though the occasion is a typical one for the explanations given by political scientists.

It is equally clear that many explanations in sociology, or in the other social sciences, are not directly about actions at all, either those of individuals or of groups. These explanations are about changes in statistical regularities or changes in social trends: changes, for example, in the Australian mortality rate from natural causes between 1900 and 1965, changes in American expenditure on funerals, changes in the size of the Negro family, changes in Glasgow rates of juvenile delinquency. All these changes—or the absence of such changes—may be explicable as the consequences of the activities of many individual people and of many organizations. The changes, or their absence, nevertheless, are not brought about by people aiming to produce them. Indeed, many consequences are the exact opposite of what the agents intended to produce, as when the passengers of a sinking boat try to save themselves by rushing to the higher side and only succeed in capsizing the craft by their weight. Or consider the vast economic power exercised in various American states by the Defense Department in Washington. No one may have intended to bring about this situation, and any explanation of its presence and rapid growth would not be a rationalistic one. Despite this, we might be able to account for the award of any given defence contract by means of a rationalistic explanation.

In general, then, there is, as Foldes says, a great range of social behaviour to which rationalistic explanation does not apply because it is not logically appropriate. This behaviour includes: errors, mistakes, miscalculations, customary practices, ritual observances, habits, automatic responses, and some convention-governed activities like growing a beard and wearing a nose ring. It is true, of course, that some of this survives because its outcome is similar to that of rational behaviour. There is also a considerable amount of social activity for which rationalistic explanation is unnecessary because both the reasons for the sake of which the activity was performed and the means employed are inescapably obvious to members of the society in question. Department stores hold annual sales in order to clear away unwanted stocks; a traffic policeman holds up his hand in a certain way when he wants the traffic to stop; a business firm raises prices after granting a wage increase because the increase has adversely affected the desired margin of profit. Cases such as these usually require no explanation of any kind except to a complete outsider. Yet these are the cases for which it is easiest to supply information about people's actual goals and the means they use in pursuit of them. In brief, rationalistic explanation is often easiest to apply when it is least needed.

It is an interesting point that when Foldes raises, as a counter-example to Harsanyi's thesis, the case of the 'relative constancy of income shares' by different economic groups—for that does not seem to admit of rationalistic explanation—Harsanyi's reply is this: 'such explanation will remain highly incomplete so long as these empirical regularities have not been explained in terms of some characteristics of individual behaviour.'[1] But what reason have we for resting content with individual characteristics? Harsanyi gives none except to say that if we wish to understand the social forces which produce, maintain, and modify such regularities, 'we are very likely to find that they require a largely game-theoretical balance-of-power model for their explanation.'[2]

However, this kind of explanation is incomplete in the same way as the explanation which it supplants. The services that determine a person's social status, for example, are themselves largely determined by social norms. Thus attaching importance to the services provided by poets is an evaluation not shared by all societies. If we are to explain why a group of people in one society give a high social status to poets whereas other groups in other societies do not, then we must answer by referring to people's adherence to the social norms and traditions of those different societies, that is, by referring to a system of conventions which account for those people's means and goals being as they are. In turn, the presence of these conventions will require explanation, for some purposes, in terms of the behaviour, needs, and interest of individual agents; and so on indefinitely. Social norms without agents are as logically impossible as social agents

[1] *Ibid.*, p. 347.　　　　[2] *Ibid.*, p. 348.

without norms, for without norms or conventions there would be no society. Because we do have societies, we necessarily must be able to explain 'some characteristics of individual behaviour' as either illustrations or consequences of non-rational adherence to social conventions. Similarly, the presence of these conventions must—logically must—be explicable as the joint outcome of the activity of agents, individual or corporate. Which member of this linked pair a sociologist uses in explanation will depend upon which of them he takes his problem to set as the explicandum—conventions or individual characteristics.

Harsanyi's treatment of the question 'How are we to explain the origin and persistence of social norms, rules, and conventions?' is not much developed. Yet this is an important issue since, as Foldes remarks, rationalistic explanations make constant and essential reference to social norms. Wanting to buy a house, for example, is wanting to obtain a house in a certain socially organized transaction between buyer and seller. Harsanyi wishes, apparently, to explain 'the existence of these social norms themselves in terms of the personal objectives and interests of the individual members of the society'.[1] He has in mind situations in which all members realize that they will benefit from mutual co-operation, and know also that their agreement to co-operate will be self-enforcing; that is, have sanctions attached to violations.

The difficulty here is twofold. A social rule—for example, the law against polyandry in Australia—may or may not have its origin in some people's 'objectives and interests'. If the law grew from traditional religious practice, the law may be simply a remnant of that practice. Moreover, that practice itself may be the unintended outcome of earlier practices or activities, rational and non-rational. And if co-operation in a given activity, as in a wedding party, is the result merely of social conformity—done because that is what is done here —it can hardly be concluded that the co-operation is explicable, rationally, as the outcome of desires to conform to tradition. The conformers may have no such desire, any more than because they shake hands with someone, they have a desire to conform to the custom of shaking hands.

Suppose, however, that we wish to explain the *persistence* or *maintenance* of a social norm rather than its origin. Here again we may have no need of individual goals and interests. It is enough for the persistence of many conventions that they exist. Even if they produce much discomfort and hardship so that no one now alive can benefit from them, they may linger on. Of course their continued existence may become the unconscious goal of some people's actions, and become so merely because those people find all old rules

[1] *Ibid.*, p. 313.

K

135

security-inducing. But while their actions are goal-directed, their sort of conservative interest does not seem to be a case of an interest whose existence is to be explained in terms of game-theory.

There is, for our purposes, a more important feature of rationalistic explanations than any of the features so far mentioned. It is that rationalistic explanations do not in themselves provide us with any new, independent laws of human behaviour. To explain an agent's behaviour as an example of rational goal-seeking, whether he uses game-theory or not, is to explain his behaviour in terms of his own reasons and his own intended actions. The explanation consists in showing (1) that the agent had a certain goal and certain beliefs about the appropriate means to it, (2) that he conducted an argument which connected that goal and those beliefs, and (3) that his belief in the soundness of that argument *caused* his action—his belief was at least a necessary part of one condition that was sufficient in the circumstances to produce the action. In giving such an explanation we are not, in its assertion, stating any laws, for the three conditions listed do not contain them. It is clear that the third condition *relies* on the truth of an unstated generalization which justifies the claim that the agent's particular belief caused his action. But this reliance indicates that a rationalistic explanation depends essentially on the existence of laws that appropriately connect belief-types with action-types, although the explanation itself does not supply these laws.

It is clear, also, that such explanations often lead us to try to produce other laws. For in testing the correctness of the reasons given by the agent for his action, we can wonder whether there are law-like regularities which connect certain sorts of agents with certain sorts of goals and with particular methods of achieving them. We can ask about the truth correlation between these agents' beliefs and their actions; the degree of the correlation, whether high or low, may need to be explained in terms of a law-like generalization linking their accuracy and truthfulness with certain additional properties of these agents. Thus while laws cannot be found in rationalistic explanations, the scientific use of such explanations both assumes and leads to a search for laws. The further question whether these laws will be social ones cannot be answered in advance. There is no methodological barrier to at least some of them being about the social rather than the individual properties of individual agents, since we have every reason to think, for example, that the goals pursued by agents, and the means employed in that pursuit, are affected very greatly by the social environment. In short, then, it is sensible to look for social laws about rational behaviour in much the same way as for any other kind of rule-guided behaviour: not as identical with the rule-following activity itself, but in the social circumstances within which that activity arises and persists, or within which it fails to arise and fails to persist.

3. Emergent and irreducible group-properties?

With our reference to the social rather than the individual properties of individual agents, we come to the other great schism between sociological theories. It is that between those which take social groups to be subject to at least some laws that are neither logically equivalent to, nor entailed by, laws concerning the behaviour of inter-acting individuals, and those theories which take all such macro-laws to be 'reducible' to laws about the behaviour of individual people. The first view is often, but not always, joined to the additional claim that at least some of the activity of individual agents, or even of identifiable agents, should be explained by macro-laws, laws which describe both the institutional roles of these agents and the functions, within the social system, of the institutions made up of those roles. The view that there are irreducible macro-laws obviously depends on the truth of another belief: that social groups possess some irreducible group-properties which either (a) can be observed and measured independently of observing and measuring the properties of group members, or (b) are essential elements of hypotheses confirmed by reference to those individual properties. The question whether sociologists should be looking for macro-laws in addition to, or instead of, micro-laws returns us to our earlier concern, in chapter three, with pseudo-properties. For the familiar problem now confronting us turns on the distinction between apparent and genuine properties. One way, then, of putting the problem is this: 'Do human groups have properties that are distinct from the properties possessed by the individual members of those groups?'

Now one favourite answer to this question has been 'Yes'; social groups have features (or properties) which are the remoter consequences of the unintended consequences of the actions performed by individual agents. Such properties are not reducible to the properties of any set of observable actions by individual people— even when we allow for the observable but unintended consequences of these actions. For group-properties, the answer continues, are called 'emergent' because their descriptions are not deducible from the descriptions of the properties of individual agents. Because of this lack of deducibility, knowledge of the properties of individuals does not permit us to predict the nature of their group's properties. In this sense, the latter are irreducible. They are emergent because they are unpredictable and hence unforeseeable and surprising. Given a set of individual people, we simply do not know, according to this answer, what kind of group will emerge. That is to say, we do not know what properties the group, taken as a unit, will have. For this reason we must take up the two questions whose answer will account for non-deducibility. The first is 'Are there emergent group-properties?', and the second is 'If so, why are they irreducible to the properties of individuals?' Both these questions can be clarified if we apply some familiar distinctions to them. We distinguish amongst: (1) Statements about the *individual properties* of individual agents. These properties are those which can be characterized without referring to the owner's membership in any social group, in any given group, or in any particular kind of group. Examples are: being able to wish to have a drink of water, being able to hope that tomorrow will bring colder weather, being disposed to expect other areas to be uncomfortable, having a good memory for interrupted tasks, having one hand stronger than the other, weighing more than 100 pounds, and believing that all snakes are dangerous. (2) Statements about the *social properties* of individual agents. These are properties whose characterization requires reference to the owner's membership in some social group, in some given group, or in some particular kind of group. Examples are: being socially deviant, being held in contempt, being Australian Prime Minister, being best man at a brother's wedding, having the largest income in the country, having a high school education. (3) Statements about the properties of groups themselves: for instance, groups of people. Examples of *group-properties* are numerical size, proportion of English speakers, and being a member of the Security Council of the United Nations.

It is important to know whether an *emergent* group-property is irreducible to individual properties or irreducible to social properties. The first suggestion is indisputably correct but uninteresting; the second is more interesting but also more disputable. The reason for the first suggestion being true is simple. Group-properties are, by definition, those properties which characterize a group because it is a collection of members who are related to each other in specific ways. It is these relations which make them members of the same groups: for example, the Hell-Fire Club. The existence of some individuals standing in these relationships is a logically necessary condition for the existence of the group and its properties. Individual properties, in contrast, are those qualities and relations which characterize an individual independently of his participation in specific, identifiable kinds of groups. Hence, given these characterizations, it is logically impossible for any statements describing individual properties to entail, *by themselves*, any statements describing group-properties, emergent or otherwise. For such a deduction to be possible our premises will have to include statements which tell us how to construct group-properties from the properties of group members. But if we admit such 'bridging' statements then deducibility is assured, and non-deducibility cannot be the test of emergent group-properties. If we do not admit 'bridging' statements, then our conclusions will not follow, since they will contain expressions (for group-properties) that do not appear in our premises. Thus, no law statements about individual properties will allow us, in the absence of 'bridging' generalizations, to predict or explain—by means of a deductive scheme—the existence of group-properties. This trivial conclusion of logic is interesting only because it is sometimes confused with another conclusion: that no law statements about *social* properties will allow us, in the absence of bridging generalizations, to predict or explain the existence of group-properties. We have good reasons for thinking *this* conclusion to be false.

Consider the example of Mr McMahon, as Australian Prime Minister, signing an order. Here knowledge of a statement about two social properties (being Australian Prime Minister and being authorized to sign governmental orders) allows us to deduce a statement about a group-property, namely, that the Australian Government gave legal effect to a previous decision. Another example is the deduction from 'Each man in this battalion tried to desert during that battle' to 'This battalion had low morale during that battle.' The first statement refers to a social property of each man—trying to desert his battalion during that battle—the second statement to a group-property—this battalion's low morale during that battle; and the first entails the second. It is true, of course, that from statements about group-properties we cannot validly deduce statements about the social properties of particular agents. Because a battalion had low morale it does not follow that every, or indeed any, man in it tried to desert. There are many ways in which low morale can be expressed. But this lack of entailment is not at issue in the question whether there are emergent group-properties. What is of interest in this connection is whether there are some group-properties that are not reducible to the social properties of the members of those groups.

However, since a group-property is emergent if and only if the assertion of its existence is not entailed by some set of statements about the social properties of the group constituents, a group-property can be emergent with respect to one such set and not with respect to another. In brief, as scientific theories about the social properties possessed by constituent agents alter, so do the group-properties which can be predicted from those theories. So in asking whether some emergent group-properties exist we may be asking whether: (a) such properties are permanently irreducible to the social properties of their constituents, or if (b) such properties are irreducible, at present, to known social properties of their constituents. The latter question is not of much interest to us *here*. For if emergent group-properties were merely those which were irreducible, at present, to known social properties of their constituents, then social groups now endowed with independent power because of their emergent properties might lose this power when a new theory about their constituent's agents was established; properties formerly emergent might change into non-emergent ones, with a consequent change in the independent power of the affected social groups. This is not a plausible interpretation of the thesis that there are emergent group-properties. The thesis must maintain that at least some group-properties are permanently irreducible, that there are some group-properties whose characterizations will never be entailed by any set of statements about the social properties of their constituents. But can such a strong claim possibly be correct?

To establish now that some—but which?—group-properties are permanently irreducible to the social properties of the group-members we need one of two sorts of argument. We must show either that the reduction is logically impermissible or that there are empirical reasons now known to us which make it forever unlikely. The second alternative would require that we now be able to predict rationally the course of all relevant future scientific theories about the social properties of constituent agents. But in order to predict the existence of those new social properties we should need to predict now the formulation of all those future theories. Yet in that case our very success would ensure that they were no longer *future* theories, contra hypothesis, and there would be nothing left to predict. Have we, then, any good reason to believe that no relevant theories now remain to be discovered or formulated? Clearly not. Hence new social properties may well appear. Since they may do so, we cannot rationally conclude that we now have good *empirical* grounds for thinking the reduction of group-properties to social properties to be forever unlikely.[1]

The first alternative is somewhat better. Either it maintains that there is a special set of group-properties whose irreducibility must be ascribed to certain logical features, or it maintains that each case is distinctive in the logical reasons for its irreducibility. If each case is distinctive, then we must wait upon the appearance of supposed cases of irreducibility. Yet what reasons have we for thinking that each case *is* distinctive? What sorts of logical features could make each case different? The reason why group-properties are not reducible to individual properties is the same in all cases. Should it not be equally so for social properties?

At this point it is important to distinguish between: (a) the *logical*

---

[1] See Sir Karl Popper, *The Poverty of Historicism*, London, 1957, pp. ix-xi; and Quentin Gibson, 'The Limits of Social Prediction', *Monist*, 52, 3, July 1968, especially pp. 370–3.

dependence of statements about group-properties on statements about the social properties of constituents, (b) the *causal* dependence of group-behaviour upon the social behaviour of the group's members, and (c) the *methodological* thesis that all law-like explanations of group-behaviour can and should be (or should not be) superseded, in the long run, by explanations referring to the law-like social behaviour of individual members. Each of these views can properly be held independently of the other two. Some attempts to identify a supposed syndrome, group-paranoia for example, as a group-property that emerges, unheralded and unrecognized, from the properties of group-members, suggest that the group-property is taken to be causally independent, in part, of the properties of individuals; the latter kind of property will be a necessary but not sufficient condition for the presence of the former.

However, the non-deducibility criterion of emergent properties—a criterion which must exclude 'bridging' statements if it is not to be trivial—offers us a logical independence whose basis is obscure. The basis cannot be that of (partial) causal independence between group and individual properties. For then the irreducibility of emergent group-properties becomes, once again, an empirical claim based on a supposed ability to predict rationally the future course of certain areas of scientific knowledge. On the other hand, the methodological thesis can only be held if we allow 'bridging' statements. These statements will relate the two classes of predicates, those referring to group-properties and those referring to the social properties of constituents, in some law-like way. That is, the generalizations will state causal connections between what are agreed to be two different kinds of properties. Once we exclude 'bridging' statements, and with them the methodological thesis, we also leave unanswered the question 'How are *explanations* in terms of group-properties related to those in terms of individuals' properties?' The basis of irreducibility must be non-empirical, and we are returned to the problem as exemplified by such supposed properties as group-paranoia.

Have we, now, any reason of logic for thinking, what may well be true, that group-paranoia is not merely a social summary of common individual paranoia? There may be no logical barrier to the truth of this negative claim, and so it may be simply an empirical question whether group-paranoia can exist in the absence of all individual paranoia. Perhaps under certain conditions a group of people who are separately unsuspicious and trustful can form a group whose group-behaviour is paranoiac. Yet here we must be careful. For if there is no logical barrier to group-paranoia *not* being merely a social summary of common individual paranoia, is there any logical barrier to group-paranoia *being* a mere social summary? Suppose every member of a newly formed group is known, from his previous history, to be a paranoiac. Are there logical considerations that would make it either self-contradictory or nonsensical for us to claim that the interaction of these individual paranoiacs produced group-behaviour which was paranoiac? Without empirical investigation, have we any way of knowing whether, and when, group-paranoia is a mathematical function of the paranoia of individual members, and hence a function of one of their *social* properties?

But obviously some properties ascribable to groups (traits of collectives) cannot be ascribed to their individual members, and conversely. Instances of the former are: crime rate per thousand people, degree of bureaucratization, volume of retail trade, and public ownership of banks. Instances of the latter are: being last person in line, being Lord Chief Justice, and being the only nurse present. In all these instances there are logical barriers to interchanging the two sorts of properties. The sense in which a city can have a high crime rate per thousand people is clearly different from the sense in which an individual person might display a high rate of criminal activity. And being the only nurse present is not something that can be either said sensibly, or verified, of a group of people.

Nevertheless, many properties ascribable only to individuals are *social* properties; their characterizations embody ineradicable reference to such membership features as being the sole occupant of a role or being the sole agent in a particular kind of situation. Therefore, group-properties are ascribed, improperly, to social individuals: for example, a statement about a city's crime rate per thousand is not entailed by statements about the crime rate per thousand of various individuals. What *does* entail the first statement, of course, is a set of statements completing, for each person in the city, the property ascription 'X number of crimes committed'. So group-properties irreducible to the identical social properties may still be reducible to *other* social properties. The crime rate per thousand people is reducible to the social property called 'number of crimes committed', assuming that the number is known for each member of the city, and hence that every member of the city is counted. It is easy to believe, wrongly, that irreducibility to the *same social* property ensures irreducibility to different social properties.

Even if it were true that group-paranoia is logically irreducible to individual paranoia, it would not follow that group-paranoia is logically irreducible to other social properties.

In point of fact, we are often not supplied with the information necessary for deciding whether a particular group-property is logically irreducible in either of these two ways. We are not told enough, for example, about the logical relationships between the notions of being a paranoiac group and being a member of such a group. The conditions for being an individual shareholder in a company and being a member of a shareholding group are different. Yet the expression 'shareholder' refers to the same property whether the shareholder is an individual or a group. Is this also true of 'paranoia'? If it is, then the relation between statements about group paranoia and statements about individual paranoia is one of logical irreducibility: the latter do not entail the former, any more than 'Every member of Group A is a shareholder' entails 'Group A is a shareholder'. But this irreducibility does not prevent entailment of the latter by a statement about other social properties. An example is, 'Every member of Group A has authorized its Financial Secretary to continue purchasing shares on his behalf, and to continue to manage and sell them in common with those of all other members, present and future.' This statement gives us something of the necessary and sufficient conditions for an individual to be a member of a shareholding group. It tells us, then, something vital about the logical relationship between 'shareholding group' and 'member of shareholding group'. We need similar information about group-paranoia. What, for example, is the difference between a paranoiac group and a group in which many members are paranoiac? If the same property-names are to be used of both individuals and groups, we need to be able to recognize, directly or indirectly, the differences between group manifestations of the properties and their instantiation by individuals. Until we can recognize the differences we have no good reason to assert the existence of group-paranoia as distinct from that of individual paranoia.

This conclusion can be applied quite generally. Social scientists often wish to ascribe properties to groups of people. Some of these properties are transferred from those ascribed to individuals: intentions, hopes, fears, wishes, motives, and moods are typical examples. Some properties like social stratification and fertility rate are not. Both kinds, however, raise the question 'How is this group-property related to the social properties of this group's members?' The point of interest, in each case, is whether we have an empirical theory about the interaction of social properties—as distinct from a definitional relationship between group and social properties—which will entail statements about group-properties. Sometimes we have and sometimes we have not. In the latter case, the irreducibility of the group-property arises from an absence of suitable premises about social properties. This absence is sometimes remedied by the recognition of previously unnoticed social properties and their interactions. Quite commonly, this occurs because we notice, or think we recognize, new group-properties (like cohesiveness, relevance, and locomotion) and adjust our notions of social properties accordingly.

But suppose, as in the case of our suggested property called 'group-paranoia', we are given insufficient information about the social behaviour of members of the group. Then we have no way of deciding whether or not the proposed property is a group-trait. The proposal may refer merely to a social property displayed in a prominent part of the group—either by a number of important members or by a significant proportion of ordinary members.

The question cannot be settled simply by our learning that the group-trait is observable, or measurable, independently of any observation of the reactions among members. Many group-traits are independently observable or measurable though they are reducible to the social properties of group-members. Thus group-shareholding, speed of committee-decision, and the loudness of choir-singing are each observable independently. Each, however, is known to be a group-outcome and so reducible to the various types of social behaviour displayed by its members. Nor is it a necessary condition for the existence of a group-property that it be independently observable; a group's morale is not observable independently of the behaviour of its members, yet this by itself does not show that morale is not a group-property. Of course, some group-properties, like some properties of constituents, are not thought to be observable at all—given the current state of knowledge of the subject. Such properties have to be inferred from evidence, as group-paranoia might be. But a large part of this evidence will usually consist in what is admitted to be observable, namely, certain social properties of group-members. The other part can consist in other, non-observable, social properties: for instance, the number of slander and libel suits brought by members whose group is said to be paranoiac. Any lack of information at a given time about these social properties will become a lack of evidence about the existence of the group-property. And a continuing lack of such information will result in a continuing doubt as to the existence of the supposed group-property.

Until this doubt is removed, it is idle for us to worry about the testability of statements ascribing the supposed property to particular groups. For we must first know how to test for the presence of the property in groups. If we cannot distinguish, either directly or indirectly, group-paranoia from the paranoia of individual members, there is no point in claiming that we can test the statement, 'Poland is suffering from group-paranoia'. We shall not know what it is that we can test. Perhaps we can test only for widespread individual paranoia. In order for the group-property to be identifiable by us, it must be connected, in a systematic way, with other identifiable properties, and this means that we must be able to discriminate between each of them and the group-property. Again, in order for us to determine whether a supposed property of any kind is genuine or not, we have to discover whether its existence produces any alteration in certain other properties, an alteration which, in the case of a supposedly irreducible property, must be not only characteristically produced by it but also unique to it. If a supposed group-property is genuine, the group to which it belongs must interact differently with other groups, or individuals, from the manner in which a group merely seeming to possess that particular property interacts with them. This difference in result allows us to distinguish, within specific situations, between a genuine and a fictitious property. It also allows us to identify the presence of the property without regard to the errors of any given observer, since a genuine property can belong to a group whether an observer thinks so or not.

The answer to the question whether there are emergent group-properties is 'Yes, but emergent in an uninteresting sense'. There is a related problem which is more important to the social scientist. That problem is the one which we have been discussing: 'How can I tell, in any given situation, whether an apparent property, or set of properties, is genuine? How can I tell whether group-paranoia or group-euphoria or status hierarchy really exist? Perhaps I am the victim of non-referring phrases; or perhaps I am merely re-christening properties that belong to individual members of these groups. Assuming that there are group-properties, whether reducible in some sense or not, how can I recognize or test for them as against recognizing or testing for the social properties of the members?' Once we seriously confront this problem, we shall find that it confers on the question of emergent group-properties most of that question's interest for the sociologist.

Chapter eight

1. Where should social laws be sought?

The question underlying our previous discussion of group-properties and social properties is 'Where ought we to look for social laws?' Our answer, so far, has been: 'Among both sorts of properties indifferently; into which one we look first matters less than our being clear about its relationships to the other.' We must now elaborate on the consequences of this answer.

It has become clear that the logical reducibility or non-reducibility of statements about group-properties need be of no special interest to the sociologist. It will not be of interest as long as there are no logical barriers to the making of law statements about group-properties; and we have seen that there are none. The reducibility of such statements is another issue. For once the possibility of genuine group-properties is assured, the fact that they are or are not logically dependent on certain social properties need not matter to the investigator. It is the genuineness of properties which makes them eligible for inclusion in a genuine law, not their logical irreducibility. The methodological thesis that all statements referring to group-properties should be reduced to statements that refer to other sorts of properties is a thesis which requires additional argument. In any case, the thesis does not bear on the question where we should look for laws. The thesis bears only on the question 'What form will the basic laws of sociology take?' And unless the sociologist has some reason for wanting to confine his search to these basic laws alone, he is free to search for laws which, in the end, may turn out to be reducible by one method or another. It may be a fact that sometimes we cannot predict the existence of a group-property from our current knowledge of social properties. But this does not show that our search for group-properties and group-laws must fail. There are more direct ways of identifying and describing them than by their connection with social properties.

Thus in looking for social laws we are entitled to seek laws concerning either social or group-properties. We are entitled also, of course, to seek laws about the individual properties of people, but in doing this we shall be practising psychology and not sociology. And if without ourselves seeking them we merely make use of such laws in the explanation of social behaviour, then while we may be doing sociology or social psychology our explanations will not be sociological in any distinctive sense. We shall be applying psychological laws to people in a social setting, and thus giving credence to the popular view[1] that there are not specifically social laws, only specifically social conditions within which certain psychological laws operate. Then our problem will be to demonstrate that the laws which account for social behaviour do not themselves contain any reference to social or group properties. All reference to them must be contained in the statements of initial conditions: that is, in the description of the particular situations to which the laws are applied.

It was pointed out earlier that statements about individual properties cannot entail, by themselves, any statements referring to group-properties. The same logical gap exists, for the same reason, between statements about individual properties and statements which refer to social properties. There can be no deduction of expressions referring to the latter if those expressions are absent from the premises. Yet supporters of the view that sociological explanation must rely on psychological laws alone commonly propose laws that refer to *social* properties, as in the case of Freudian generalizations about the Oedipus complex, sibling rivalry, the origin of feelings of guilt, shame, and envy; or as in social psychologists' theories about leadership, power, conformity, status, and competition. For example, we might try to explain 'the extensiveness of menstrual taboos observed in a primitive society' in terms of 'the average intensity of castration anxiety felt by men in that society'.[2] Generalizations of this kind are, at best, laws of *social* psychology. If they are not to be called 'sociological generalizations', then the claim that there are no sociological law-statements is merely the claim that there are no laws about group-properties. The chief *logical* reason for holding this view, however, is a reluctance to believe in the possible existence of group-properties, and this reluctance is not well founded. Hence,

[1] See, for example, G. C. Homans, 'The Relevance of Psychology to the Explanation of Social Phenomena', in *Explanation in the Behavioural Sciences*, ed. R. Borger and F. Cioffi, Cambridge, 1970, pp. 313–28.
[2] W. N. Stephens, 'A Cross-Cultural Study of Menstrual Taboos', in *Cross-Cultural Approaches*, ed. C. S. Ford, New Haven, 1967, p. 69.

147

critics of sociological laws must think either that *laws* about group-properties are unlikely to be found for empirical reasons or that there are no laws concerning social properties. Each of these conclusions has its difficulties, since each will require us to predict what we cannot know—the outcome of future scientific theories. For as we have seen, there are no logical barriers to laws about group-properties; and, equally, there can be none to the existence of laws about social properties—unless we are prepared to argue that so-called social properties do not exist. But who would be prepared to assert that being a lawyer is not a social property, that its characterization does not depend upon the person's membership in a certain kind of society, a society which has a formal legal system?

Nevertheless, there is also a problem connected with the discovery of laws about social properties. The problem is that social properties arise, to a large extent, from the rule-governed activities in which members of social groups participate. When we look for laws connecting social properties with one another we must be careful to distinguish, as before, between regularities and laws. Many social properties are connected by the regularities of behaviour that result, directly or indirectly, from rule-following. These constant associations between social properties are not themselves laws. Thus we know that the joint presence of the two social properties of being an employer and being a racial discriminator does not vary inversely with the presence of the social property 'being able to evaluate easily the performance of employees'. We also know that the property of being a member of a disliked and helpless minority is not invariably associated with the property 'being an object of displaced aggression by the majority'. The presence of other properties is required, even though we may not be able to state them. The partial association between being a minority member and being the object of majority aggression is merely a regularity of social behaviour and not a full-fledged causal relation. In short, our attempt to discover law-like relations between social properties raises all the problems previously discussed under the heading 'explanation of behaviour in terms of rule-observance and rule-violation'. The attempt does so because all rule-observance is behaviour with social properties: that is, behaviour which the agent only displays because he is a member of a particular group or a particular sort of group. Much rule-violating behaviour does not meet this condition, of course, for much of it appears simply because the agent is *not* a member of a particular sort of group—is not a pacifist, for example, and so does not renounce the use of force in dealing with difficult social problems. But some rule-violations occur because the agent is a member of a particular sort of group and thus has certain social properties. In these cases the explanation of his behaviour will take the same form as rule-observance, and hence raise similar questions about the invariable links between social properties.

Of course, not all social properties are displayed in rule-observances and rule-violations. There are social properties like being sexually promiscuous or jealous or honest which may issue in spontaneous, rare, idiosyncratic, unintended, or unforeseen behaviour. All of it may be unregulated by any conventions in the agent's society. When this is so, our attempt to find law-like relations between these social properties and other social properties does not run the common danger of mistaking rules for laws. Instead, we run the opposite danger of thinking that merely because the behaviour is not rule-governed it is not explicable by means of social laws. We may think that because there is no convention about the most suitable season of the year in which to obtain a divorce, the large rise in the divorce rate of last winter has no law-like social explanation; or perhaps requires no explanation except that of showing the rise to be only apparent or only an unintended consequence. In practice, it is easy for the same people to fall into both errors, since anyone who is likely to mistake regularities for laws is likely, in consequence, to mistake the absence of regularities for the absence of laws.

We have been arguing that sociologists are logically entitled to look for social laws which connect either social or group-properties. To this we must now add that sociologists are entitled, also, to search for social laws that connect social with group-properties. The cohesiveness of a social group may be increased if all its members have the same level of social prestige outside the group. The joint output of a work group may decline if members with the same skills are rewarded differently. The officers of an army battalion may strengthen its morale by making themselves more accessible to complaints from their men. The fact that some statements about group-properties are deducible from some statements about social properties is not, in itself, a good reason for avoiding the use of the former, any more than the reducibility of some laws of chemistry to those of physics makes the chemical laws redundant. To know that a certain group-property can be reduced to certain social properties is useful information. But for any one of various reasons it does not follow that the group-property can be usefully eliminated from our discussion about social life. That will depend both on the nature of our problem and how we propose to use its solution. If our groups exhibit independent, stable behaviour over long periods, and are clearly marked off from each other, we may think that, for some problems, the groups' interaction is best explained by treating them as observable units. However, we must remember what many of our previous examples have shown: that law-statements about groups are exposed to the same sorts of difficulties as law-statements about the social properties of individuals. The common alternation of falsity and triviality in both kinds of statement is proof that changing the property-type is not a solution to these difficulties.

2. Do sociologists need help in finding laws?

Now sociologists wish to know something of the sorts of laws for which they are logically entitled to search. But both they and their critics have much more interest in actual prospects than in mere logical entitlements. Sociologists are concerned with the sorts of laws which they are most likely to discover—given that conditions in their field are as we have described them. Can we say anything helpful about these sorts? Can we do more than try to lay out the logical boundaries? The answer, obviously, is that suggestions, like more formal hypotheses, are the indispensable prerequisite of later criticism. If we value the potential benefits of such criticism, then we must favour whatever makes it possible.

Perhaps the most important point to be made about such suggestions is that, strictly speaking, they are not needed. To put them forward is to assume that sociologists are commonly in the position of having many good problems which require solutions in terms of laws, and that sociologists, for some reason or other, do not know where these laws are most likely to be found. Neither of these assumptions is true. On the contrary, a large proportion of sociological problems are so ill-formed that they can never receive a useful solution. And of those which are well-formed, a large pro- portion do not require an independent law-explanation but some other sort: for example, one in terms of rule-following or rational goal-seeking. Of those well-formed problems which do demand law-explanations, it is not correct to say that their authors need help in determining where those laws are to be sought. The problems themselves provide this information, since it is not possible to formulate a clear, specific question without knowing what *sort* of reply will count as a satisfactory answer. But knowing what *sort* will count as an appropriate kind of answer here is the same as knowing what kind of law to look for; that is, the area in which the required law is likely to be found, if it can be found at all.

Consider the following example taken from A. R. Lindesmith's book *Addiction and Opiates*.[1] He there distinguishes between 'addic- tion' and 'habituation'. The former term refers to 'behaviour which is distinguished primarily by an intense conscious desire for the drug, and by a tendency to relapse, evidently caused by the per- sistence of attitudes established in the early stages of addiction'.[2] The latter term refers to 'the prolonged use of opiates and to the

[1] Chicago, 1968.   [2] *Ibid.*, p. 64.

appearance of tolerance and withdrawal distress, when it is not accompanied by the behaviour described above as addiction behaviour'.[1] Habituation is necessary but not sufficient for addiction. The problem, as Lindesmith states it, is 'that of isolating the factors which account for the transition from a biological condition, induced by regular drug administration for a period of time, to a psychological state of addiction or craving'.[2] He then describes three cases which show that craving does not follow from physical dependence alone, that the subject's knowledge that he is using an addictive drug is not sufficient to produce his addiction, and that self-administration of the drug is neither necessary nor sufficient for addiction.[3] Lindesmith goes on to say that given the presence of physical dependence (habituation), the three cases suggest 'that a critical and universal feature of addiction is the recognition and proper identification of the withdrawal distress'.[4] He concludes that addiction does not come from the drug's initial euphoric effects, 'but from the beginner's realization that the discomfort and misery of withdrawal is caused by the absence of the drug and can be dispelled almost magically by another dose of it'.[5] Thus repeated doses establish the addiction by a process of negative reinforcement: in the beginning they simply remove the unpleasant symptoms; later on the doses anticipate the symptoms and prevent them from appearing.[6] The factor which turns habituation into addiction is the subject's identification of his withdrawal symptoms. The law which determines the onset of addiction is the joint presence in the subject of habituation and recognition of his own withdrawal symptoms.

In this example, the factor being sought has to account for the difference between physical dependence, whether conscious or unconscious, and conscious addiction or craving. According to the theory, the factor is a piece of causal information obtained by the subject, namely, that his distress can be removed by the consumption of a certain drug. Becoming addicted is learning how to eliminate or avoid withdrawal symptoms by the use of that drug.

Now given the formulation of the problem—to explain the subject's change from habituation to addiction—it is clear that the factor being sought has to explain the appearance in the subject of a new desire for a specific drug. The subject had come to know that he wanted the drug, and the investigator could not account for the existence of the new desire without also accounting for the change in the subject's information or belief, since that change was a necessary condition of the new desire. The investigator's question then became, 'What new information (or belief) led the subject to desire the drug?' And the answer hit upon was 'His belief that the

---

[1] *Ibid.*, p. 65.   [2] *Ibid.*   [3] *Ibid.*, p. 73.   [4] *Ibid.*
[5] *Ibid.*, p. 74.   [6] *Ibid.*

L

drug would eliminate his distress'. The fact that the drug did relieve his distress then led the subject to continue its use.

This example shows us how the phrasing of a problem narrows the field of plausible answers to a particular area, the area in which, in this case, the missing portion of the required law was likely to be found. The example also shows us how inferior to this process would be any general answer to the question 'Where ought sociologists to look for laws?' For it would not be helpful to say, 'Look at changes in people's beliefs and desires'. We already know that such changes partially determine the changes in people's actions. Any less general reply would require us to know the specific problems at issue, and if we knew those we should not need the reply itself.

If drug-addiction is a form of pain-avoidance, then addiction is usually, though not always, rational in the short run and irrational in the long run. It is rational in the short run because it does eliminate withdrawal symptoms. It is usually somewhat irrational in the long run for two reasons that are closely related. One is that the subject's future supply of his drug is commonly not assured. The other reason is that he tends to increase his consumption so far beyond the needs of bodily comfort or efficiency as to produce physical discomfort and deterioration. This additional dose, although thought to be necessary by the addict, is not in fact missed by him if it is secretly withdrawn. The addiction process thus presents us with two different sorts of problems and, hence, with a need for two different sorts of answers.

The first problem is why the subject craves a certain minimum amount of his drug at regular intervals. The answer is that he believes, correctly, that the dosage will eliminate or prevent his withdrawal symptoms. This explanation is 'rationalistic' because it refers to the agent's conscious attempt to achieve a clear-cut goal by reasonable means. The second problem is why the subject craves an additional and increasingly larger amount of his drug at regular intervals. Here the explanation is not 'rationalistic', for the increased consumption is both compulsive and ill-adapted to achieving the avoidance of pain in the long run. The subject's knowledge of these deficiencies does not prevent him from increasing his consumption. Lindesmith explains this behaviour as the outcome of the subject's increasing familiarity with his own withdrawal symptoms:[1]

> he learns to detect the very first signs; these warn him of future distress, and as a result is inclined to magnify their extent and importance. He feels sicker than he really is, and since he regulates the time of each injection by the way he feels, he is impelled to use the drug sooner than otherwise. Then, having taken the dose prematurely, he finds that he does not 'feel the

[1] *Ibid.*, p. 91.

shot' as he did the last time. The effects of an injection are
noticed in proportion to the contrast between the states *before*
and *after* the dose takes effect; it follows, then, that in order to
'feel his shot' the addict must now increase the size of the
dose . . . The process is further promoted by the tendency of
the organism to adapt itself to doses of any size.

This account tells us that the compulsive increase of dosage is
caused by an increasing sensitivity to anticipated pain; that the
anxiety then produced leads to an error in judgment concerning the
state of the withdrawal symptoms and to a consequent early dosage;
that the early dosage does not produce the anticipated and desired
effect; and that the subject regularly increases his dose because he
believes, correctly, that by this means he will regularly receive the
desired effect. By attempting to correct, repeatedly, for an initial
error, the subject constantly magnifies its consequences by a process
of positive feedback which he is unable to stop. His behaviour is
goal-seeking but not rational, since his activity is explained in terms
of a causal compulsion to obtain a certain effect.

This explanation is a causal account of an unintended consequence
(constantly increasing dosage). But the properties referred to in
addiction—the withdrawal symptoms, the effects of the injection,
the increased sensitivity to anticipated pain—are only individual
(physiological or psychological) properties, and not social or group
properties. For this reason, it may be suggested that the case is
different with problems whose answers refer to the latter two sorts of
properties; that problems concerning them do not narrow the field
of plausible answers to an area in which the required law is likely to
be found. Yet the basis of this suggestion is not clear. The basis may
be the methodological view that there are no laws connecting social
or group properties. On this view we have already argued, first, that
there are no logical barriers to such laws and, second, that the results
of future empirical work cannot be known in such a way as to rule
out the likelihood of these laws. On the other hand, the basis of the
suggestion may be merely that, for some unknown reason, questions
which make essential reference to social or group-properties do not
allow us to narrow the field of plausible answers in a satisfactory way.
This view is obviously implausible unless supported by the previous
one. In any case, it is false that reference to social or group properties
has this consequence, and the following two examples will make the
point plain.

In their book *Black Rage*,[1] two American psychiatrists raise the
question why, among adolescent Negro girls in the United States,
there is an unusually high frequency of obesity. Their suggestion is

[1] By W. H. Grier and P. M. Cobbs, New York, 1969.

that the obesity is only one symptom of these girls' 'abandonment of youthful narcissism and the associated competition for male attention'.[1] This process continues in adult life: 'In their thirties and forties they seem to give up competition for male interest. They neglect their figures . . . concern themselves more with the utility of their clothing and less with style, and resign themselves to a relatively asexual maternal role in which work and a hovering concern for the family occupies them entirely.'[2] What the authors wish to explain, therefore, is not simply the high frequency of obesity among adolescent Negro girls, but the high frequency of a certain sort of obesity, that due to a more general neglect of personal appearance among Negro women of certain ages. This neglect demands explanation because non-Negro women of the same economic level in the same society devote much attention to improving their personal appearance. How are we to account for this difference?

The authors of *Black Rage* give three reasons.[3] One is that the American ideal of feminine white beauty is physically impossible for Negro women to achieve, and that their own Negro features are thought to be ugly and repulsive by the white population; and in consequence, by Negro women themselves. The second reason is that until recently physical beauty in black women was a dangerous quality, since it attracted casual sexual advances by white men. This danger has been replaced, for the ghetto girl, by that of similar advances from brutalized black men. The third reason concerns the relationship between the weakened narcissism of black women and the low esteem in which they are held by black men.[4]

There is a natural inclination for a woman to yield herself to a powerful lover, gaining additional narcissistic supplies in her possession of him. Her own high evaluation of herself, in turn, evokes in the man a similar high evaluation of her. If her narcissism is impaired, the sexual act is a degrading submission to a man who does not value her, and she arises from it feeling a loss of self-esteem rather than a personal enhancement.

Given these circumstances, young Negro women have found it impossible to achieve a satisfactory level of sexual relationships, and they have turned their attention elsewhere—to protecting, rearing and educating their children.

This account says that American Negro women are prevented by various social circumstances from achieving certain goals. When the women realize that success is impossible, they abandon all goals of that type; and with them are abandoned all the behaviour and interests appropriate to obtaining them. Pursuit of a different sort

---

[1] *Ibid.*, p. 39.   [2] *Ibid.*   [3] *Ibid.*, pp. 39–44.
[4] *Ibid.*, p. 42.

of goal is substituted: the enhancement of the women's appearance is replaced by enhancement of their children's welfare.

Now whatever the explanatory merits of this account, it contains both a reference to social properties and an indication of the field of plausible answers. The social properties include: believing oneself to be ugly, being especially subject, as a member of a minority group, to casual sexual advances, and holding oneself in low esteem. The field of plausible answers is marked out by the phrasing of the original question—'Why do so many more young Negro than young white women neglect their personal appearance?'—and by the assumptions from which the question arises. The most important of these assumptions by the authors are that (a) the difference in response of the two groups is the result of *social* factors which operate in one group and not in the other, and (b) there are psychological grounds for believing that the factors operate in the case of most women, so that it is the case of the Negro women which is aberrant and needs to be explained. When these assumptions are joined with the view that the white women are pursuing a goal from which the Negro women have turned away, the explanation of the difference must lie in some condition which acts as a deterrent to the latter. This deterrent, the authors suggest, is the belief of Negro women that they are irremediably ugly and of little value except as mothers.

The source of this belief is to be found in the three conditions just described. They prevent or punish the goal-seeking behaviour in question rather than reward it. Since the means available to the women have little chance of producing success—for hair-straightening and skin-bleaching have obvious limitations—it is reasonable of black women to give up the pursuit of Caucasian standards of feminine beauty. But it is not reasonable of them to neglect their appearance for this reason alone without further thought, because even if they believe those to be the only worth-while standards, neglect of appearance is not the only alternative to trying to achieve them. This explanation, then, like the previous one, takes the form of describing the explicandum (neglect of appearance) as a partly unintended consequence of a rational activity: in this case, that of substitution of goals. The consequence is *partly* unintended, according to the second reason, because black women realize the dangers of their pursuit of personal beauty and inhibit themselves appropriately.

Explanations in terms of group-properties display the same kind of linkage between question and answer as do explanations which refer to individual or social properties. The following example drawn from Jane Jacobs's book, *The Death and Life of Great American Cities*,[1] will show this. Suppose we learn that the rates of

[1] Penguin, 1964.

street crime—such crimes as armed robbery, assault, and rape—vary considerably among different streets in the same city. Suppose we also learn that these rates vary greatly among different cities in the same country. We learn that:[1]

> Los Angeles, for example, has a forcible-rape rate (1958 figures) of 31·9 per 100,000 population, more than twice as high as either of the next two cities, which happen to be St. Louis and Philadelphia; three times as high as the rate of 10·1 for Chicago, and more than four times as high as the rate of 7·4 for New York.
> The overall Los Angeles rate for major crimes is 2,507·6 per 100,000 people, far ahead of St. Louis and Houston, which come next with 1,634·5 and 1,541·1, and of New York and Chicago, which have rates of 1,145·3 and 943·5.

In addition, assume that we hold, as part of our stock of relevant beliefs, these two: (1) '. . . that the public peace—the sidewalk and street peace—of cities is not kept primarily by the police, necessary as police are. It is kept primarily by an intricate, almost unconscious, network of voluntary controls and standards among the people themselves, and enforced by the people themselves.'[2] (2) 'that the problem of insecurity cannot be solved by spreading people out more thinly, trading the characteristics of cities for the characteristics of suburbs. If this could solve danger on the city streets, then Los Angeles should be a safe city, because superficially Los Angeles is almost all suburban. It has virtually no districts compact enough to qualify as dense city areas'.[3]

Now having these beliefs and pieces of information, we may then be led to ask, as Jacobs does, whether *part* of the difference in crime rates cannot be accounted for by the difference in criminal opportunities offered by different kinds of streets. That is, we begin by assuming that the public peace is kept on only those streets which allow the 'network of voluntary controls' to operate. Our question, therefore, must be 'What street conditions are both necessary and sufficient, in the circumstances, for the operation of voluntary controls?' A successful answer to this question will tell us, in part, why some streets have low rates of crime and other streets have high rates. By extension, the answer will tell us, also, why these rates vary from city to city. For the answer will be that the cities vary in the number and proportion of their streets which have the control-maintaining conditions.

What, then, are these conditions? Jacobs offers three. 'First, there must be a clear demarcation between what is public space and what is private space. Public and private spaces cannot ooze into each

[1] *Ibid.*, p. 42.   [2] *Ibid.*, p. 41.   [3] *Ibid.*, pp. 41–2.

other as they do typically in suburban settings or projects.'[1] The reason why this condition is necessary is that people must be willing to assume and ascribe responsibility for actions. They will not do this, and so voluntary controls cannot operate, if the line between private and public responsibility is blurred. It becomes blurred when people's limited and voluntary participation in street life develops into an intrusion of their private lives. If people's privacy is seriously threatened, they withdraw completely from casual friendliness and co-operation. As a result, they no longer help to support the 'network of voluntary control' which keeps the streets safe.[2]

> Second, there must be eyes upon the street, eyes belonging to those we might call the natural proprietors of the street. The buildings on a street equipped to handle strangers and to ensure the safety of both residents and strangers must be oriented to the street. They cannot turn their backs or blank sides on it and leave it blind.
> And third, the sidewalk must have users on it fairly continuously, both to add to the number of effective eyes on the street and to induce the people in buildings along the street to watch the sidewalk in sufficient numbers. Nobody enjoys sitting on a stoop or looking out a window at an empty street. Almost nobody does such a thing. Large numbers of people entertain themselves, off and on, by watching street activity.

These three conditions are said to be the properties which a street, that is, a traffic passageway with associated buildings and people, must have in order to be safe from street crime. The properties, as given, belong to a place, but they can easily be redescribed so as to apply to the group of people in that place. Instead of 'public space' we can write 'group space'; and for 'proprietorial eyes' and 'side-walk watchers' we can substitute 'group-informants'. It is the group of people living on a street who display a higher or lower degree of surveillance and maintenance of public peace, even though their success or failure is determined by reference to a geographical location, namely the street which the people occupy.

It is obvious that the answer to the question whether the three conditions are necessary, or sufficient, or both, depends upon the content of a number of unstated assumptions. They refer to certain social conditions that prevail in large American cities, but we are not told by Jacobs which of these conditions are presupposed by her explanation. Because we do not know this, we do not know whether her three conditions are supposed to hold only of large American cities, or of all large cities with specifiable features, or of all large

[1] p. 45.
[2] *Ibid.*

cities in general. Our ignorance does not affect our present purpose
except in so far as we are made cautious in claiming that Jacobs's
original question not only narrowed the field of plausible answers
satisfactorily, but also narrowed the field to one in which a required
law was likely to be found. For since we do not know whether her
three conditions are advanced as the full statement of a social law
or merely as some part of it, we cannot know whether other important factors in the desired law should not be sought elsewhere. It is
easy to imagine, for instance, that a street's crime rate might rise
sharply if the street suddenly began to be used by a group of people
who were traditional enemies of the residents.

The original question was 'What street conditions are both
necessary and sufficient, in the circumstances, for the operation of
voluntary controls?' This question assumed the truth of the law-like
statement that the public peace of large cities 'is kept primarily by
an intricate, almost unconscious, network of voluntary controls and
standards among the people themselves, and enforced by the people
themselves'. The answer consists in trying to show that there is
something of a law-like connection between the presence of this
network and the presence of three conditions: assumption of
responsibility for public space, proprietary surveillance, and street
activity sufficient to ensure that surveillance. These conditions are
important in causally maintaining the network. If this answer can
be made good, then its author will have provided us with a social law
which can be used to explain both the presence of street crime and
variations in its amount.

But whether or not the answer is correct, it was well localized by
the original question. For operation of voluntary controls logically
requires that the participants be informed and willing. The explanation that is offered by Jacobs simply describes the actual circumstances of street life in which those two requirements are met. That
is, once the truth of the statement about voluntary controls was
accepted, it became important to ask, first, what their logically
necessary conditions are and, second, under what actual circumstances these logically necessary conditions make their appearance.
To be informed about street life we require the presence of street
watchers; and to have responsible street watchers we must circum-
scribe their area of responsibility by clearly marking off public from
private space. The difficulty for the sociologist does not lie in
discovering that the presence of informed and willing participants
is a logically necessary condition for the presence of voluntary
control. It is obvious that the statement 'Voluntary control is present'
logically implies the statement 'Informed and willing participants
are present'. The difficulty lies in discovering under what circumstances of street life the occupants are both informed and willing.

Since from Jacobs's original information we can logically infer that informed and willing participants must be present, her question comes closer to telling us what kind of law to look for—one concerning the conditions in which such participants are present—than could any general principle about the procedures of searching and finding.

Chapter nine

1. A summary of the basic argument

In chapters one and two it was suggested that there are, in sociology, certain non-theoretical terms to which it has proven difficult to give useful criteria of application. These terms include 'discrimination', 'minority', 'prejudice', 'alienation', 'delinquent', 'relative deprivation', and many others. A detailed examination was made of the difficulties connected with trying to provide sociologically useful criteria for one of them—'discrimination'. These are criteria which would allow us to apply the term correctly to recognizable cases and to measure their incidence.

The source of such difficulties, it was argued, is that such terms are implicitly relational; they embody the notion of observable divergence from a particular social standard, a standard which varies according to the policy judgments adopted by different people in different societies. Only when we specify a particular standard do the criteria give us a means of picking out the exemplifications of a relation, a means of recognizing certain relational properties. In brief, the terms are 'policy-dependent'. The distinction between a dictionary definition of a policy-dependent term like 'discrimination' and a sociologically useful one is the distinction between a lexical definition of a relation-term and a stipulative definition of a relational-property term. Since our operational criteria for policy-dependent terms must specify the standard being employed on each occasion of their use, it is logically impossible to give general criteria for, and thus to measure, discrimination or delinquency or prejudice or alienation *per se*. It is not possible to give a single operational specification of—a single criterion for—the many different aims and contents of all the various social standards which the use of a policy-dependent term can presuppose.

The search for satisfactory operational specifications can also be described as an attempt to produce definitions which refer to measurable properties of scientific interest. In chapter three this search was discussed in terms of two examples: first, the relationship between prejudice and the authoritarian personality, and second, the relationship among anomie, authoritarianism, and ethnocentrism. It was argued that because the authoritarian personality is not a natural kind, it cannot be treated as a single variable, and hence that there can be no possible causal connection between it, taken as one variable (or property), and any second property—for example, that of prejudice. Attempts to treat prejudice itself as a complex property with three dimensions—cognitive, emotional, evaluative—were criticized in turn as being incoherent. For none of these three dimensions, it was argued, is a natural kind (or complex property) which can causally affect the other two dimensions or affect other properties. Not only does none of the dimensions form a constant cluster of tightly associated properties, but the different dimensions include some of the same features. This confused classification and description of the features of prejudice make it useless for correlation with the authoritarian personality, just as the latter's deficiencies as a variable make it an unsuitable correlate of prejudice.

The difficulty of providing operational specifications for the terms 'authoritarian personality' and 'prejudice' was taken as an illustration of a widespread tendency, the tendency of sociologists to bring together as the names of variables a motley host of terms. In doing this, sociologists often fail to make three important distinctions: (a) generic *v.* specific dispositions, (b) specific dispositions *v.* their exemplifying episodes, (c) tendencies *v.* capacities. By overlooking these distinctions, sociologists have been led into indiscriminate correlations of variables, and thence into unjustifiable inferences about the relationships holding among them.

Srole's study of anomie, authoritarianism, and ethnocentrism is a case in point. For the account he gives of anomie straddles the question whether 'anomie' is the name of a social dysfunction or the name of an agent's psychological isolation. The evidence produced in his study will not support the first alternative. But the second is no better, since when we define 'anomie' solely in terms of an agent's beliefs we lose the link with social dysfunction and make it impossible to predict the agent's behaviour. Nor can we test the empirical content of claims about anomie; and hence cannot determine whether the term refers to a genuine process or state. It is pointless, then, to try to correlate the incidence of anomie, so defined, with either authoritarianism or ethnocentrism. The criteria of application used for 'anomie' are basically unsatisfactory.

Inadequate criteria of application for a term have, as one of their common consequences, the untestability of statements in which the

161

term appears. The production of adequate criteria for terms is closely connected with success in formulating the problem to which the terms are relevant. Chapter four dealt with some of the hazards of problem-formulation. The examples given earlier of ill-formed questions, pseudo-statements, and untestable theories were generated, it was suggested, by a common misuse of variable analysis as a method of sociological investigation: the method, that is, of establishing and analysing correlations of variables where the distribution of the variables is determined by surveys or questionnaires. The misuse arises, it was said, both from lack of constraints on what is to count as a variable, and from the attempt, in the absence of any directly relevant theoretical background, to discover causally significant correlations. Without such a background we run two dangers: (1) our criteria of application—operational specifications—are drawn either from common sense or covert hypotheses; our problem is thus formulated in terms of unexamined, and perhaps false, assumptions; (2) most of the high correlations we find will be of no scientific interest because they are not related to any reputable hypothesis or theory. We cannot discover sociological laws by mere correlation-hunting even though testable hypotheses seem to be in short supply. Yet why should there be such a scarcity? Is it a genuine one? These are two of the questions to which chapter five was directed.

A very large number of sociological generalizations are commonly said to be either plainly false or tautologous. Blalock's examples of statistical generalizations about discrimination illustrate the force of this charge. For these generalizations, like many others in sociology, give us only the initial conditions under which some unknown, law-like generalizations are thought to hold. These initial conditions can be defended only by turning the statements in which they appear into analytic truths. To account for this oscillation between falsity and tautology we must become clear about the relationship between social laws and social rules. And this requires us first to be clear about the character of social laws.

We need to distinguish between accidental and nomological generalizations; between empirical and theoretical generalizations; between universal generalizations and probabilistic generalizations. In the case of the first distinction, nomological generalizations (statements of law) assert a hypothetical relation, an invariable connection, whether or not the relation is actually exemplified. Thus statements of law support, as accidental generalizations do not, subjunctive and counterfactual conditional statements. Most universal statements about social practices are accidental generalizations and not statements of law. For most such statements of social practices are not supported by any accepted theory. Yet they bar hypothetical cases which these theories would admit.

The importance, for sociologists, of distinguishing empirical from theoretical generalizations is that sociologists often confuse accidental universal generalizations with empirical universal generalizations. Both of the latter two are generalizations from observed regularities, and it is often unclear whether or not the generalization is a genuine observational law. A theoretical law, in contrast, contains descriptive terms which do not appear in the statements used to test it—terms which have no direct observational or experimental procedures for their use. A theoretical statement of law is not open to direct testing by observed instances, for the sense of some of its terms is given indirectly by the theory to which it belongs. The weak development of useful theoretical laws in sociology has two unfortunate consequences: (a) it becomes difficult to distinguish empirical laws from accidental generalizations, since we cannot use either theoretical support or subjunctive difference as tests; (b) we do not have systematic connections among the empirical generalizations which were established independently of each other; their explanatory scope and ability to generate proposals for new generalizations are correspondingly restricted.

The sociological significance of distinguishing universal from probabilistic (or statistical) laws arises from the constantly recurring need to determine whether a probabilistic causal connection can be inferred from a particular correlation of variables. The most important difference between statements of universal and statistical laws is that from the latter nothing is entailed about any finite set of instances of the reference class. Therefore the use of statistical laws for explanation or prediction gives only an inductive conclusion; and testing of these law-statements is difficult. However, most sociological generalizations are, and are likely to continue to be, statistical in character. For the sorts of questions which sociologists ask are derived from problems that are phrased in our everyday vocabulary. The terms of this vocabulary refer to classes of non-homogeneous members. The generalizations which connect such classes are thus bound to be statistical. But if sociologists greatly refined their vocabulary, they would run the danger of achieving successful universal generalizations at the cost of altering the problems on which the generalizations were originally supposed to bear.

The oscillation, in sociology, between generalizations which are obviously false and those which are tautologous can now be accounted for in part. Much of the oscillation is due to sociologists confusing the search for social laws about rule-oriented behaviour with the misguided search for law-like causal rules. Social rules and regularities, it was argued, are neither social laws nor exemplifications of such laws. Nor should social laws or social rules be identified with the various kinds of regular results of rule-oriented behaviour: rule-

163

embodiments, intended and natural consequences, unintended effects. If we do not separate all these one from the other, we are likely to mistake social rules, social regularities, social practices, and their causal consequences, for loose laws—'quasi-laws'—as do Helmer and Rescher.

In chapter six some of Blalock's generalizations concerning discrimination in employment were used as examples of the difficulty of distinguishing, in actual situations, between social rules, social regularities, social practices, and genuine social laws. The difficulties were found to be these: (1) when policy-dependent terms are used, we cannot recognize instances of the properties to which they refer. In order to pick out classes of recognizable members, and to produce law-like statements connecting those classes, we require the additional information which a policy judgment supplies. Any statement of law, then, which used policy-dependent terms would have to specify, in each case, the particular factors on which a given policy, and hence the use of the corresponding term, was based. The result would be, at best, a long list of quite specific, and thus not very useful, statements; (2) there is often uncertainty as to the character of the explicandum and how to describe it; (3) there is also a more general factor, namely, the tendency of sociologists constantly to try to widen the scope of their generalizations; in doing this they expose themselves even more to the problems created by the needs of testing, the use of policy-dependent terms, and the uncertainties of characterization.

There is also another general problem: how the scarcity of plausible law-claims is related to the sociologists' concentration on certain kinds of topics and questions. Why, then, do so many of the sociologists' questions and procedures ensure the discovery of social regularities rather than social laws?

Much of the subject matter of sociology consists in the rule-oriented behaviour of people. Much of the sociologists' attention, therefore, is fixed on such behaviour and on its regular consequences. Sociologists use the presence of these social regularities to explain particular pieces of group behaviour. Policy-dependent terms, for instance, are used to refer to the rule-oriented behaviour of a particular social group. Hence, the answer to our question is that the sociologists' questions and procedures are commonly, but not always, about the regularities of rule-oriented behaviour. Sometimes, however, the sociologists are interested in explaining rule-violating behaviour. When they are, they must explain why the rules were not effectively observed. Usually the answer is that some necessary condition for successful rule-following was not met. But sometimes the breaches require explanation in terms of the agents' observance of different rules and the pursuit of different ends.

164

Yet sociologists must also explain the presence, origin, operation, need for, and success of, social rules or conventions themselves. This must be done in terms of statements of law. Furthermore, some social behaviour is not regulated by rules or conventions. It is to be explained as the unanticipated consequences of rule-oriented behaviour, or as the causal consequences of the agents' conformity to conflicting conventions, or to the effects on social institutions of new technological and commercial practices, or to the results of disasters on social life.

The concentration by sociologists on rule-oriented behaviour, rather than on social laws or law-explanations, does not mean that the search for social laws is pointless. Nor does it mean that sociological generalization is impossible, that the shortage of plausible generalizations indicates that there really are no social laws, and hence no successful explanation with their aid.

But in what aspects of social life should sociologists be looking for law-governed behaviour? The answer, taken up in chapters seven and eight, has usually been phrased in terms of two major divisions between theories of social behaviour: (a) the division between rationalistic and non-rationalistic theories, (b) the division between theories concerning individual agents and theories concerning groups. (a) was discussed first. Clearly, much social behaviour, whether individual or corporate, is not rationally goal-directed. Moreover, many sociological explanations are not about either individual or group action. They are about changes in statistical regularities or changes in social trends. In addition, it is logically inappropriate to use rationalistic explanation for such things as: errors, Freudian mistakes, miscalculations, customs, rituals, habits, automatic responses, and some convention-guided activities. Rationalistic explanation makes constant and essential reference to social rules. Yet their origin and persistence often cannot be given a rationalistic explanation, one in terms of the agent's goals and his beliefs about the means to achieve them. Nor does rationalistic explanation supply any new independent laws of human behaviour. Instead, it depends essentially on, and leads to a search for, the existence of laws connecting types of beliefs with types of actions. Some of these laws may be about the social, rather than the individual, properties of agents. In brief, it is sensible for sociologists to look for social laws about rational behaviour—as for any other kind of rule-oriented behaviour—in the social conditions in which the behaviour arises and persists, or fails to arise and fails to persist.

The second division between theories about individual agents and theories about groups raises these questions: 'Do human groups have properties distinct from the properties possessed by individual members of those groups? Are laws about social groups "reducible", in some sense, to laws about the behaviour of individual agents?' To answer these questions we must begin by distinguishing three types of properties—individual, social, and group. The last of these, it was argued, are irreducible to the individual properties of individual agents. The more interesting question, however, is whether any group properties are permanently irreducible to the social properties of individuals. To this it was replied that some group properties are irreducible because we do not have the required empirical theories about the inter-action of social properties, theories which entail the desired statements about group properties. The conclusion was drawn that sociologists are free to look for social laws about either social or group properties, or for laws connecting the two types.

Chapter eight continued to inquire about which areas of social life sociologists might profitably examine for social laws. Many critics have denied the existence of such laws, and have claimed that sociology must rely on psychological laws. But these critics have usually proposed, as 'psychological', laws that refer to the social properties of individual agents; and such laws cannot be entailed, for reasons given earlier, by statements about individual properties alone. The so-called 'psychological' laws are at best laws of social, not individual, psychology if we are not allowed to call them 'social laws'. The claim that there can be no social laws is then merely the claim that there can be no laws about group properties. This claim is not well founded.

When we seek laws connecting social properties with one another we must separate, as always, regularities from laws. Many social properties are connected by the regularities of behaviour consequent upon rule-following. These regularities of behaviour are not themselves law-like. But while all rule-observance is social behaviour, not all social behaviour is rule-observance. We must not suppose that non-rule-governed behaviour cannot be explained in terms of social laws. We must neither mistake social regularities for social laws, nor the absence of social regularities for the absence of social laws.

So far we have been pointing out logical entitlements. Can we do more than that? Can we suggest to sociologists, in more detail, where they ought to look for social laws? The answer is 'no'. For if a sociologist has a well-formed problem which requires a law-explanation, the problem itself will show him where to seek the answer. It will show him what sort of answer will count as a satisfactory one: that is, what kind of law to seek. Thus Lindesmith's theory of drug addiction, the Grier-Cobbs hypothesis about obesity in Negro girls, and Jacobs's treatment of the rates of variation in street crime, all show us how the phrasing of a problem, and the assumptions from which it arises, narrow the field of plausible answers—whether the properties in question are group, individual, or social ones. What we are shown is much superior to any general answer to the question 'Where ought sociologists to seek social laws?' For only attempts to solve specific problems can specify the actual causal conditions in which the logical requirements of the guiding hypothesis are realized. No merely general principle about searching and finding procedures can tell us that much.

2. Context-dependence, comparable social units, and generalizations of law

By now it will be obvious that the problem with which we began in chapter one—that of finding criteria of application for such policy-dependent terms as 'discrimination'—is only one example of a more general task. That task is to construct a descriptive vocabulary which will permit a cross-cultural comparison of the main features of human social life. The need for appropriate definitions of the terms of this vocabulary has often been stressed. A. R. Radcliffe-Brown, for example, once wrote that sociologists had not really dealt with 'the difficulty of defining what is meant by the term "a society".' He develops his objection thus:[1]

> They do commonly talk of societies as if they were
> distinguishable, discrete entities, as, for example, when we are
> told that society is an organism. Is the British Empire a society,
> or a collection of societies? Is a Chinese village a society, or is
> it merely a fragment of the Republic of China? If we say that
> our subject is the study and comparison of human societies, we
> ought to be able to say what are the unit entities with which we
> are concerned.

The same point has been made many times about such common and basic terms as 'sibling', 'family', 'descent', 'marriage', 'tribe', 'clan', 'religion', 'political state', 'magical practice', 'legal system', and 'relative'. Each of these—and many other—sociological terms refers to a large number of quite different social arrangements. If we use such terms to generalize about a class of societies, in the sense of correlating two or more social practices, we find that the weakness of our statistical correlation simply reflects the basic diversity of the properties to which each term refers. Thus 'matriliny' is the sociologist's term for a society's placing of people into kinship classes in terms of their descent traced through women. These classes, as D. F.

[1] 'On Social Structure', *Journal of the Royal Anthropological Institute*, 70, 1940, pp. 4–5.

Aberle pointed out,[1] may take many forms, whether or not organized into lineages, sub-clans, or clans. The kinship classes may or may not be concerned with such activities as defence, inheritance, and hospitality. The kinship group may be geographically widespread or its members may live together in the same place. Hence, said Aberle, 'When we ask under what conditions matriliny is found, we seem to be attempting to account simultaneously for the conditions which create and those which perpetuate a wide variety of types of units lumped together solely by the pattern of descent reckoning.'[2]

Now it is clear that in complaining of 'a wide variety of units lumped together' or of the 'diversity of the properties to which each term refers', we are simply asserting that certain terms—'matriliny' and 'society' for example—do not provide us with categories whose items are homogeneous enough for certain purposes of generalization. It is the purposes for which they are to be used that determine whether or not they are *homogeneous enough*, of course, for any possible set of items will be homogeneous in *some* respects. It is only some similarities which are relevant to, and hence useful for, our purpose; and it is only those which we wish our definitions to mention or to imply. The familiar problem of defining the term 'marriage' is a case in point, since much of the discussion of that question neglects to say to what sociological uses the required definition is to be put: that is, to what sorts of generalizations and theories the definition is thought to be relevant. Merely 'isolating the phenomenon' will not answer this question.

E. R. Leach began a well-known controversy on the definition of 'marriage' by asserting that 'marriage is (to borrow Maine's phrase) "a bundle of rights"; hence all universal definitions of marriage are vain.'[3] E. K. Gough defended the opposing view and suggested this definition: 'Marriage is a relationship between a woman and one or more other persons, which provides that a child born to the woman under circumstances not prohibited by the rules of the relationship, is accorded full birth-status rights common to normal members of his society or social stratum.'[4] The most obvious feature of this proposal is that it picks out, but does not characterize, only one of the many classes of rights created by marriage. The definition says nothing, for example, about many of the rights listed by Leach: sexual monopoly, rights to labour and property, rights

---

[1] 'Matrilineal Descent in Cross Cultural Perspective' in *Matrilineal Kinship*, ed. D. M. Schneider and E. K. Gough, Berkeley, 1961, pp. 656–7. As quoted in W. Goldschmidt, *Comparative Functionalism*, Berkeley, 1966, pp. 28–9.
[2] *Ibid.*, p. 29.
[3] *Rethinking Anthropology*, London, 1961, p. 105.
[4] 'The Nayars and The Definition of Marriage', *Journal of the Royal Anthropological Institute*, 89, 1959, p. 32.

168

between relatives of the marriage partners.[1] Nor does the definition indicate the various activities which married parents characteristically engage in concerning their children: their nurture, education, and future well-being. Leach had written: 'in no single society can marriage serve to establish all these types of rights simultaneously; nor is there any one of these rights which is invariably established by marriage in every known society.'[2] Gough replied that the phrase 'full birth status rights' is an abbreviation for 'all the social relationships, property rights, etc. which a child acquires at birth by virtue of his legitimacy'.[3] Which of these a child acquires will depend upon the particular society into which he is born. The defining property of marriage for Gough, then, is the presence of the concept of 'legally established paternity', and hence the possible rights acquired by the child through the socially recognized legitimacy of his birth. Now this definition may or may not hold generally. It is an empirical question whether in every society marriage confers status rights on the children. Leach instances polyandry among the Sinhalese as a counter-example. He says: it is 'not concerned with the rights of the potential children. The marriage rite disposes of the woman's sexuality to her first husband; it also has the effect of making a public pronouncement that the woman has been properly endowered so that she has no further claims on her parental property. The status of children arises from quite a different source.'[4]

What is of interest to us here is that the definition of 'marriage' raises problems similar, in some ways, to those created by the definition of 'discrimination'. The lexical definitions of both are very general and fail to provide operational specifications for particular instances. The reason is the same in both cases. Both terms are context-dependent, and so are the respective families of terms which they represent: policy-dependent terms like 'delinquent', 'social deviant', and 'prejudice' which embody judgments of value; and terms like 'family', 'society', 'religion' which do not. Policy-dependent terms are only one, though an important, kind of context-dependent term. Other kinds are represented by such terms as 'here' and 'now', or 'light' and 'large', or 'better' and 'worse'—or, as in the present instance, 'cousin' and 'father'. Just as 'here' means 'in this place' where 'this' refers to the speaker, and 'worse' means 'worse in some (unspecified) respect', so 'marriage' refers to a socially acknowledged relationship which creates some unspecified sub-set of a long list of rights and duties. Which ones are created in any given case depends upon the particular society in which it occurs. Of course, the features which make up the marriage practices of one community may vary so greatly from those of another that we may be uncertain whether

---

[1] *Op. cit.*, pp. 107–8.   [2] *Ibid.*, p. 108.   [3] *Op. cit.*, p. 32.
[4] *Ibid.*, p. 112.

to call both practices 'marriage'. Is common-law cohabitation a form of marriage? Not if Gough is correct. Is Sinhalese polyandry not marriage but only plural mating? It is marriage if Leach is correct. Borderline questions such as these can only be settled by definitions drawn up with an eye to the other purposes which the definitions are to serve. Settling *all* borderline issues by means of one definition of a term is not itself an appropriate goal, of course, since each definition is liable to create new borderline questions.

When context-dependent terms are employed with no indication of context, they are always ambiguous and usually vague. They are ambiguous in that they do not indicate exactly which members of a set of properties or objects are being referred to; and are usually vague because the boundaries of the set must remain open to the influence of new contexts. New kinds of marriage-like relations, for example, may be invented or be discovered to exist. In such a situation there may be advantages in our being able to classify them as marriages rather than as something else, and the vagueness of the term 'marriage' may permit us to do this without difficulty. On the other hand, in using context-dependent terms to describe social institutions and relationships, the sociologist is ensuring that his problems in making cross-cultural comparisons, and in establishing law-like generalizations, will be acute.

There is another factor which creates difficulties for sociological description: it is the use of culture-bound terms. Any sociologist, like any social anthropologist, must *begin* his investigation of at least some social behaviour, whether the behaviour be that of individual people or groups, by trying to understand its point for the agents: that is, he must try to grasp what it is they are trying to do or bring about. In order to do this—to learn their intentions—the investigator must understand what the agents' own account of their goals, reasons, motives, intentions, and actions would be. He must know what the agents take themselves to be trying to accomplish, how they would describe their actions if circumstances permitted. In brief, the sociologist must be familiar with the agents' own potential descriptions and explanations of their behaviour. If he were not, he would not know what they thought they were doing. But if he did not know this, he would be unable to pick out, and then account for, the actions they took themselves to be performing. Yet many actions are *defined* in terms of the agents' intentions—marriage, murder, theft, incitement, conspiracy, fraud, and contract are obvious instances. The sociologist's ignorance of his subjects' intentions, as given by their own potential descriptions, would result in his being unable to describe and explain their behaviour as actions of those kinds, as being a genuine case of marriage as against mere residential mating, for example. The sociologist's explicanda—the agents' actions—could not be described and identified; his generalizations would remained unformed.[1]

The sociologist is crucially dependent, then, upon his subjects' potential descriptions of at least some of their actions—those actions into which the agents' intentions enter as defining conditions. But these descriptions, potential and actual, will contain many culture-bound terms. That is, the members of each society will characterize their own institutions and practices in a vocabulary which evolves in step with, and caters to, local needs. It commonly does not matter to the Irish that elsewhere in the world marriage takes place without a bridesmaid or a best man. Nor does it matter to the Irish description of their own marriage practices that terms like 'bridesmaid' and 'best man' have a use only in certain societies. It matters to the comparative sociologist, however. For if he wishes to generalize about marriage practices in various societies, he will have to *begin* with local accounts of those practices, begin with the culture-bound terms in which the members of different societies describe their own practices. He will then have the task of replacing these local terms with more general ones which help him to classify together a large number of what he takes to be only superficially diverse activities. At this point he will be tempted to resort to context-dependent terms like 'marriage attendant' or 'marriage' itself. Thus in the effort to surmount the limitations imposed by culture-bound terms, the sociologist will formulate his generalizations in context-dependent terms. But the use of the latter will simply ensure the vagueness, ambiguity, and low coefficient of correlation of which sociological generalizations are so often accused. Hence, while the employment of context-dependent terms is a recipe for referring to non-homogeneous properties and objects, the use of culture-bound terms is a permanent bar to the sociologist's ability to produce law-like generalizations.

3. Explaining cross-cultural generalizations

How, then, is cross-cultural generalization to proceed? The sociologist seems to be trapped. Either he presents us with a large set of purely local studies, each described in terms of the subjects' own concepts, or he presents us with a smaller set of generalizations which oscillate, as we saw earlier, between being true but empty and false but significant. Yet the remedy, once stated, is familiar to social scientists as being transparently clear in outline—although much less clear in detail. C. G. Hempel has put the relevant point briefly: 'laws that are formulated at the observational level generally turn out to hold only approximately and within a limited range; whereas by

---

[1] For this point see A. MacIntyre, 'The Idea of a Social Science', *The Aristotelian Society*, Supplementary Vol. 41, 1967, pp. 107–11.

theoretical recourse to entities and events under the familiar surface, a much more comprehensive and exact account can be achieved.'[1] In short, the sociologist has three tasks to perform: (1) he has to learn the concepts and vocabulary (whether observational or theoretical) in terms of which his subjects try to understand that part of their own social behaviour of which they are aware; (2) he has to replace their concepts and vocabulary with ones which both embrace the subjects' unconsciously adaptive activities and advance the comparative and generalizing purposes of the sociologist; (3) he has to produce a theory—a set of inter-related theoretical laws—which accounts for his own empirical generalizations, and in doing so accounts also for his subjects' interpretation of their own practices.

Up to this point we have been concerned, for the most part, with steps (1) and (2). We have stressed, for example, the sociologist's need to understand the rules and conventions which govern the social behaviour of his subjects. We have also emphasized the importance of distinguishing among: first, the subjects' use of these conventions to describe, or explain, their own behaviour; second, the sociologist's use of these conventions to account for his subjects' behaviour; and third, the sociologist's use of law-like empirical generalizations to account for the presence or operation of both these rules and their consequences. These three activities fall within steps (1) and (2). However, the last step (3) is the most difficult one to take successfully. Not only does it presuppose the success of the previous two steps, but it requires the invention of a theoretical terminology with whose aid useful statements of law can be produced. Since this terminology and the corresponding statements of theoretical laws—theoretical generalizations—are developed hand in hand, an impediment for one is an impediment for both. We cannot fail with one and be successful with the other. For this reason, the invention of both a theoretical terminology and its accompanying generalizations may both be hampered equally if we insist on retaining some of the problem-formulations on which our original sociological interest was founded.

Suppose, for instance, that our original interest was to find answers to such ordinary questions as 'How can we eliminate poverty in our community?' 'Why does racial discrimination exist here?' 'How many social classes are there in Australia now?' We may find that the questions have to be recast before we can give them scientifically satisfactory answers. Our common-sense terms like 'poverty', 'racial discrimination', and 'social class' may be inadequate, for reasons already canvassed, to the explanatory role. Or the question may arise from a misconception, or not admit of a definite answer. Whatever the difficulty, the invention of theory may have to wait upon a change

[1] *Philosophy of Natural Science*, Englewood Cliffs, New Jersey, 1966, p. 77.

in the formulation of the problem, and hence upon a change in our earlier interest. Yet such a change may be strongly resisted, even by social scientists. For with respect to issues of social policy, an investigator may be as firmly committed to his own formulation of the problem as he is open-minded concerning its possible answers.

Nevertheless, many sociological theories, often of a common-sense kind, have been advanced in explanation of cross-cultural generalizations. It is easy to give examples of such theories, although it is often less easy to judge either their soundness or the truth of the generalizations which they try to explain. Fortunately, only the first of these tasks need be attempted here. We are interested in the general character of these theories and not in their empirical success.

One of the most popular types of such a theory is based on the view that certain social and psychological needs of human beings repeatedly call forth, in all societies, similar social problems. Each society must try to solve these, and some solutions—some institutions and customs—will be fairly common because their advantages are obvious; they are the generally preferred means of coping with similar needs. In correlating social practices drawn from different societies, we are trying to establish a correlation between similar solutions, solutions to what we think of as similar problems. But the correlations are usually weak because similar solutions can arise for different social problems, and different social solutions can be invented for similar problems. We should realize, so the argument goes, that it is certain social *problems* which are universal, and not their solutions. Once we do so, we can construct a theory based on social problems and the universal needs that they embody—rather than a theory based merely on social institutions and the diverse local solutions which they incorporate. What is theoretically important is the need which is to be met, the social requirement which is to be fulfilled, not the various organizational ways in which the job is done.

Thus the power of the state, says Goldschmidt,[1]

> may be defined by a formally drafted constitution, by an evolving set of customs embodied in a few recorded acts, by religious ideology, or by an elaborated historical myth. These may be legitimated by appeals to natural right, divine right, biological superiority, or historic mission. Power itself may be transmitted by inheritance (variously patterned), election, court revolution, or an interregnum of anarchy and the brute use of force among contenders.

But any social theory concerned with the state must account for these various institutional arrangements as different ways of coping with

[1] *Op. cit.*, p. 115.

173

three general social requirements for a state: the defining of political power, the legitimizing of that power, and its transmission to new officials. One advantage of thinking in terms of 'functional require-ments'—conditions necessary for the functioning of the system—is that we can then ask a series of empirical questions about these requirements. For example, under what circumstances are they necessary? What happens when some of them are not met? Gold-schmidt suggests that the history of African states provides many examples of what he calls 'inadequately realized political systems' with a limited life-span. By examining these we can learn the con-sequences which follow from the absence of solutions to certain political needs.[1]

For sociologists who favour this kind of theory it is natural to assume, as Goldschmidt does, that human groups usually exploit their environment as best they can, given the technology at their disposal; and that they create institutional arrangements for dealing with the ensuing needs.[2] He instances the high correlation between nomadic pastoral societies and the presence of agnatic segmentary lineages. The correlation is to be explained in terms of such kin groups being well suited to the organizational needs of pastoral economies. 'Sentiments of filiation' are enlisted, the physical abilities of men are used for animal care and military defence, especially the protection of the herds, and the lineages permit quick changes to be made from action by individuals to action by large, unified groups with central authority.[3] However, segmentary lineages are not a necessary condition of the functioning of pastoral economies. Age-sets, for example, are at least a partial substitute.[4]

The difficulty of fully stating such a theory so that it has any explanatory force is obvious. If the frequent presence of segmentary lineages in pastoral economies is explained in terms of the kin groups being a successful, but not a necessary, way of coping with certain problems, this explanation may be either rationalistic or not rationalistic. If it is the former, then we attribute to our agents a degree of rational goal-seeking in connection with the adoption, or maintenance, of segmentary lineages which is extremely implausible. If our explanation is not rationalistic, then the persistence of these lineages is the effect of their causal role in the pastoral economy. But this is only to say that their presence is explicable because they are an element in a self-persisting system: in brief, that they have a function in it. Once we admit this, however, we are faced with the familiar problem that only if a condition (segmentary lineages) is *necessary* to the preservation of a system (nomadic pastoral economy) can we begin to explain why *that* particular condition is present. If

[1] *Ibid.*, pp. 116–17.   [2] *Ibid.*, p. 121.   [3] *Ibid.*, p. 123.
[4] *Ibid.*, p. 124.

some other conditions will also serve, then we can infer only that one of these conditions must be present if the system is to survive. Which one is present will depend upon historical circumstances, and this piece of information must form part of our explanation why one, rather than another, of these conditions is present. We need, also, some additional information about which properties of the system are maintained in a steady state by segmentary lineages, how these properties are to be measured, and what are the external conditions, with their limits and values, under which the system will continue to respond to the influence of segmentary lineages. In the absence of the additional information, our claim that the lineages are an element in a self-maintaining system is an empty one. We can pick out neither the system nor the connections between it and the supposed contributing element.[1]

So far we have seen little evidence of the theoretical vocabulary and theoretical generalizations by whose means the sociologist is supposed to explain the empirical generalizations which describe the behaviour of his subjects. Terms like 'definition, legitimatization, and transmission of political power', 'segmentary lineage', 'age-set', and 'nomadic pastoral economy' are much the same terms as appear in the various empirical generalizations which are being explained. Nor are the explanatory generalizations themselves any different in type from the empirical ones. The explicandum 'Nomadic pastoral societies commonly have segmentary lineages' differs in no relevant respect from the explicans 'In nomadic pastoral societies the segmentary lineage occurs often because it provides an organized corps of men for the care and defence of the herds.'

However, it is possible, and common, to interpret the universal needs of people of all societies in psychological rather than social terms. Cross-cultural generalizations then form either the explicanda, or the predictions—and hence tests—of the psychological theory. The theoretical hypotheses and theoretical terms of the theory are used to account for and test the presence of the institutions in question. A characteristic example arises in W. N. Stephen's paper 'A Cross-Cultural Study of Menstrual Taboos'.[2] In the course of testing the hypothesis that the average intensity of male castration anxiety significantly determines the elaborateness of menstrual taboos in a society, Stephens constructed a scale for measuring the extensiveness of menstrual taboos in any given society. He then correlated the scale scores for different societies with the scores for a large number of other factors thought to be indicators of, or associated with, castration anxiety. One of these correlations was between menstrual

---

[1] For an expansion of this view of functional explanation see Brown, *op. cit.*, chapter IX.

[2] In *Cross-Cultural Approaches*, ed. C. S. Ford, New Haven, 1967.

taboo scores and scores for 'long post-partum sex taboo'. The positive relationship was statistically significant: that is, societies having a long post-partum sex taboo tended also to rank high on the menstrual taboo scale. This is, in effect, an empirical generalization about rule-guided behaviour, a generalization which might well have been discovered in a variety of ways. In fact, it was predicted as a result of the theory being employed. But how is the correlation to be explained?

The answer is as follows. A long post-partum sex taboo has the effect of displacing the mother's frustrated sexual interest on to the nursing child. This interest will sexually arouse the child and lead to an early and intense relationship with the mother. According to Freudian theory, this sexual arousal is one of the contributing conditions in childhood to the later development of intense, persistent fear of genital injury—castration anxiety. (The other two general conditions are punishment of the child for sexual activity, and severe punishment of the child for behaving as a rival of the father.) Castration anxiety determines the elaborateness of menstrual taboos, since the presence of menstruating women stimulates the unconscious male fear of genital injury to themselves. Restricting the activities of menstruating women by imposing taboos on them protects the adult men from their own largely unconscious anxiety. Hence, a long post-partum sex taboo helps to produce the adult male castration fear which, in turn, is the cause of high scores on the menstrual taboo scale. When the length of the sex taboo declines, or when the taboo is absent, the castration anxiety tends to weaken, and thus so does the strength of menstrual taboos.

Other examples of psychological explanations of cross-cultural generalizations are easily found. Thus Barbara Ayres used data from twenty-nine societies to test, and substantially confirm, 'the hypothesis that the severity of the sanctions associated with violation of food taboos [in pregnancy] will be positively related to the severity of punishment for dependent behaviour in childhood.'[1] The explanation offered for this association of severity of sanctions on following food-rules and the severity of childhood punishment for dependent behaviour is that this severity will create fear and anxiety concerning the expression of dependent behaviour; that eating is an unconscious gratification of dependency-needs and hence is subject to the adult anxiety produced by the punishment of dependent behaviour in childhood; and that severe sanctions for female violation of food taboos during pregnancy simply reflect the strength of the anxiety whose expression is to be avoided.[2]

[1] 'Pregnancy Magic: A Study of Food Taboos and Sex Avoidances', in Ford, op. cit., p. 115.
[2] Ibid., pp. 115–16.

Again, we might ask the question 'What are the child-rearing conditions that should lead to a preoccupation with parental ghosts?' If we assume that neglected children produce fantasies of nurturing parental figures, and if we also assume that these children are severely punished for aggression, we can suggest that they will become adults who fear parental ghosts at funerals. In a test of thirty-two societies J. W. M. Whiting confirmed that the three variables are positively correlated to a high degree. The correlation is accounted for both in terms of fantasies as wish-fulfilment, and in terms of the children's displacement of their aggression toward the neglectful, punishing parents on to the parents' dangerous ghosts.[1]

These three examples of explanation rely upon the theoretical vocabulary of psychology, and in particular, the theoretical vocabulary of psychoanalysis. The relevant terms include: 'wish-fulfilment fantasy', 'displacement or projection of aggression', 'drive reduction', 'dependency-wish', 'gratification of dependency', 'negative and positive fixation', 'frustration', 'anxiety', 'Oedipus complex', and 'castration anxiety'. These terms do not appear in the empirical generalizations which are being explained. Nor do such explanatory theoretical generalizations as 'A long post-partum sex taboo encourages the displacement of the mother's frustrated sexual interest on to the nursing child' and 'Eating is an unconscious gratification of dependency-needs' resemble in type the empirical generalizations for which they are used to account. Whatever the shortcomings of psychoanalytic theory, it comes near to meeting the purely formal requirement which we demand of any theory: that it refer to non-observational events and properties which can be used to explain the data of observation. Meeting this requirement is clearly not sufficient to make the psychoanalytic theory an adequate one for sociological purposes. But meeting this requirement is sufficient to distinguish psychoanalysis from those many sociological 'theories' which, unhappily, do not do so.

However, we have been at pains throughout this book to argue that no *general* sociological deficiency follows from particular defects of this kind. It would be a mistake, for example, to claim that *all* sociological terms, are, or must be, context-dependent. For to make that claim would simply be to revive the claim rejected earlier that the search for universal social laws is doomed to fail—doomed because no genuine theoretical vocabulary and theoretical generalization can, in the case of sociology, be constructed. To this the critic now adds a new reason: that all the terms which sociologists might use to form such a vocabulary are context-dependent. The reply to this objection is at once simple and familiar. It is that the critic cannot

[1] 'Sorcery, Sin, and the Superego: A Cross-Cultural Study of Some Mechanisms of Social Control', in Ford, *op. cit.*, pp. 154–9.

177

anticipate the discovery of explanatory theoretical properties. There are no logical bars to their presence, and they cannot be abolished by fiat. We can, of course, cease to look for them and thus decrease our chances of finding them. But since we can invent non-explanatory (unsuccessful) theoretical properties at will, the critic must be predicting that all future theoretical properties will be of this unsuccessful type. He must also be asserting that all those theoretical properties known to sociologists at present are similarly fruitless. The latter claim is false, and hence the former is unfounded, even if, as we have tried to show, sociologists have often confused the issue by looking for such a property in rules and rule-following rather than in the causal conditions from which rules and rule-following arise.

If the argument of the preceding chapters is correct, sociologists need not forever oscillate between the extremes of empty social generalizations and patternless ethnography. Indeed, to the contrary, in the ways we have previously described, the one extreme breeds the other; and in giving up either we abandon both for something better.

Index

179